TEEN CONFIDENCE UNLOCKED

TURN NEGATIVE BELIEFS INTO SELF WORTH, ADVERSITY INTO AUTHENTICITY, PERCEIVED WEAKNESS TO REALIZED STRENGTH, AND FEAR INTO FREEDOM

CHAD & KRISTI METCALF

EDITED BY

BRAD TEMPLE

STUDIO 5326 LLC

COPYRIGHT © 2023 BY CHAD METCALF

FREE BONUS CHAPTER - YOU WILL LOVE THIS! (FROM THE STARTING LINE TO THE EDISON MINDSET)

RESOURCE TO HELP YOU GET STARTED

The first step is often the hardest when learning something new. That's why we have created a workbook to accompany this book. You can definitely use a notebook, but sometimes it is helpful to have everything laid out. If for some reason the QR code does not work, you can find the workbook by searching Amazon.

INTRODUCTION

Have you ever felt like you're not good enough, not smart enough, or not cool enough? Are you constantly worrying about or second-guessing your looks or concerned that you don't fit in with other teenagers? If you answered "yes" to any of those questions, you're not alone. Did you know that nearly 20 percent of teenagers experience some form of depression? Did you know that 75 percent of teenage girls cope with self-esteem by smoking, drinking or starving themselves?

Although it may seem like the best thing to do is to avoid confronting the many emotions experienced during middle and high school, I assure you that you will be much better off by actively acknowledging, navigating and triumphing over these emotions. By doing so, you will emerge a more accomplished, self-assured young adult.

The truth is that your teenage years can and should be some of the best years of your life. It's a time of self-discovery and freedom from adult responsibilities. Still, the bad moments can sometimes outweigh the good, and you can't help but focus on your struggles. Teenagers struggle for many reasons, including not feeling that their parents and caregivers understand them, sibling rivalry and jealousy, and being bullied for different reasons. Being a teenager isn't easy, and I'm sure you know this. But we want to tell you that you're unique and valuable and have something extraordinary to offer the world. Although you might not feel like it, the confidence you need to live a fulfilling and incredible life is within you; you just have to unlock it.

My wife and I felt compelled to write this book to share our experiences. Experiences that we have learned firsthand from trials in our own lives and insights we have gained from raising three sons who are currently walking through the many challenges faced by middle and high schoolers today. Within the pages of this book, you will discover the invaluable tools we have used ourselves and provided to our teens, enabling them to conquer these challenges effectively. As a result, we can proudly say that they're growing into confident and capable young adults and we want the same for you.

This book provides practical strategies, advice and tips to help today's youth overcome the obstacles and difficulties that come with being a teenager. Get ready to embark on a journey of discovery as we discuss the following topics:

- What confidence is and why you need it.
- How to overcome self-doubt and change the way you think about yourself.
- Strategies to defeat low self-esteem and become more confident.
- Tips on how to improve your communication skills and become more assertive.
- How to navigate peer pressure and make the right choices.
- A step-by-step process for goal setting and goal achievement.

This is only a snippet of the life-changing information you'll have access to, and we can guarantee that it works because there are many examples to prove it.

Many of you reading this book know who Arianna Grande is and may even admire her talent, beauty and confidence. Arianna often speaks about her insecurities and what it was like growing up in front of the world. During an interview with Seventeen magazine, she said that she was so insecure about her looks that she would spend hours getting ready to take a selfie that was good enough in her mind to post on social media. Even though she got millions of likes, she focused on a minority of nasty comments.

One of the biggest life lessons Arianna learned is that it's okay not to have the answers to everything. She once wanted to know why people said terrible things about her online when she did her best to please her fans. She would spend so much time and energy worrying about other people's opinions of her that she got lost in self-doubt. Although she was massively successful, the negative comments made her forget about how talented she was and focus on her flaws. Arianna did everything she could to be perfect but still felt like it was never good enough. Now she knows that true confidence isn't about being perfect. It's about embracing your imperfections and believing in yourself. She didn't come to this conclusion overnight; she had to do a lot of self-reflection and inner work to get to the point where she was okay with being who she was.

Still not convinced? Here's an inspiring story I came across when writing this book. At 14 years old, Charlie was diagnosed with depression after being bullied for years for being overweight. Although he tried to ignore his peers, he couldn't move past the negative mindset he gained. His parents tried everything to help him, but Charlie couldn't overcome his insecurities until he watched a story on YouTube about a 16-year-old boy named Trevor who was in the same situation. He was overweight, had acne, didn't get good grades, and was bullied. Things weren't looking good for Trevor until he read a book about changing your habits to become successful. Trevor applied the principles he read, and within a year, he changed his diet, lost weight, got rid of his acne, and improved his grades. His bullies began to admire his changes, and he began teaching them what he had done to turn his life around. This story motivated Charlie to follow in Trevor's footsteps. He has also lost weight, improved his habits, made many new friends and, most importantly, learned to be confident in who he is. His example is an inspiration to others.

While I would love to guarantee an instant transformation where all your struggles vanish and you become the most confident teenager in the world overnight, I want to emphasize that life's journey toward confidence does not unfold in a single leap. It is a gradual process that requires dedication and effort. However, with each step forward and each ounce of determination you invest, you are paving the way for a brighter, more confident future. Think about what you do to pass an exam. You study for a while and then apply the information you've learned. Without applying that newfound knowledge, you won't pass the exam. Developing confidence works in the same way; you've got to apply what you learn in this book to your life. It's all in this book, it's up to you to use it, to become the confident, self-assured and fearless person you are destined to be. If you're ready to start your journey to unlocking confidence, keep reading!

CHAPTER 1

UNLEASHING THE POWER WITHIN

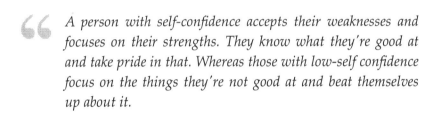 *A person with self-confidence accepts their weaknesses and focuses on their strengths. They know what they're good at and take pride in that. Whereas those with low-self confidence focus on the things they're not good at and beat themselves up about it.*

RIGHT NOW, YOU MIGHT NOT FEEL VERY CONFIDENT, AND THAT'S FINE because most teenagers don't. However, I believe every human being is born with confidence. Just think about babies; they're fearless and crawl around without a care in the world because they want to explore their environment. When they're ready to start walking, they get up and go. When they fall, they keep trying until they're confidently toddling along on their tiny feet. Babies keep trying because, deep down, they know they can do it. They are not conscious of their confidence, but they're confident. If we're born with confidence, why do so many teenagers have trouble finding it? It's because each negative life experience takes it away (more on this later). The more bad experiences we have, the less confident we become until we're a shadow of our former selves. Life is challenging, and everyone needs a healthy dose of confidence to get through it and become the best version of themselves to be an asset to the world. The good news is that your confidence isn't lost forever; it's still in you. It's just buried, and now is the time to find it again. Let's start by defining what confidence is.

WHAT IS SELF-CONFIDENCE?

According to the American Psychological Association, confidence is: "Trust in one's abilities, capacities, and judgment. "a belief that one is capable of successfully meeting the demands of a task." Basically, self-confidence is how you see yourself. It's about your beliefs and opinions of yourself. For example, when you admire someone, you respect them because of the qualities you think they possess. You might admire your older sister because she's kind, generous, clever, funny, and good at her job. If you were to look at yourself through someone else's eyes, what would you see?

Having self-confidence is an essential trait that can lead to many positive qualities. When someone is confident, they exhibit a sense of calm and assurance that radiates in everything they do, from their personal life to their professional endeavors. It allows individuals to believe in themselves, their abilities, and their decisions, leading to healthier relationships, improved communication skills, and better overall well-being.

Self-confidence can affect whether you:

- Value and like yourself as a person.
- Are assertive in making decisions.
- Believe you deserve the best in life.
- Think you're good enough.
- Believe you are valuable to the world.
- Overcome your mistakes by owning them and learning from them.
- Are kind to yourself.
- Acknowledge your strengths.

Here are some of the remarkable qualities that can be cultivated through self-confidence.

LEARN YOUR STRENGTHS

There's no such thing as perfection; it doesn't exist. You can be extremely talented, attractive and accomplished but still have flaws, and that's okay. You see, everyone has strengths and weaknesses. Some people are naturally intelligent and get the highest grades in school without putting in much effort, but they're terrible at sports. Others are very artistic; they can draw, paint and create beautiful things with their hands, but they're not good with numbers. A person with self-confidence accepts their weaknesses and focuses on their strengths. They know what they're good at and take pride in that. Whereas those with low-self confidence focus on the things they're not good at and beat themselves up about it. Self-acceptance is also about valuing yourself for who you are without the need for others' approval.

Comparing yourself to others can lower your confidence if you don't understand your strengths. Your confidence will go down if you constantly compare yourself to someone with entirely different natural gifts. This would be like a goldfish comparing itself to a squirrel and feeling like an idiot because it couldn't climb a tree. If the hypothetical goldfish just identified its own strengths, it would realize that the idea of a goldfish climbing a tree is absurd. We are no different, so figure out your strengths first. One resource I recommend is the Clifton Strengths Finder. It's a short book that also has an online test you can take to identify your top strengths. Once you know your strengths, you can use them to stack the odds in your favor and start getting your confidence back.

Assertiveness

ASSERTIVENESS IS KNOWING how to express your opinions, thoughts, needs, and boundaries clearly, confidently, and respectfully. It involves standing up for yourself and advocating for your rights and interests. Assertive people are more likely to get what they want because: 1) they're not passive; and 2) they can express their needs without being aggressive.

Resilience

Confident people don't wallow in self-pity; they understand that life is full of peaks and valleys and that important lessons must be learned when things don't go as planned. They see opportunities as obstacles and bounce back from setbacks with a positive outlook and renewed strength.

Growth Mindset

A growth mindset is about how we think and approach learning and challenges. It's about believing in your ability to improve and grow. Instead of accepting that our abilities are fixed and that we're either "good" or "bad" at something, a growth mindset tells us that we can develop and improve with practice, effort and perseverance. So let's say you're given a difficult essay for homework. You know that English isn't your best subject, and you'll struggle with it. Instead of accepting defeat because you're bad at English, a growth mindset would say, "Even though English isn't my strongest subject and this essay seems difficult, I'm confident I can get a good grade by seeking assistance and giving it my all. Making mistakes is part of the growth process, and I can only gain knowledge from this experience." A growth mindset focuses on embracing challenges as opportunities to learn and grow rather than giving up or getting discouraged.

WHY DO TEENS NEED SELF-CONFIDENCE?

Confidence is vital for teenagers. It's essential for everyone but even more so for teenagers because these are the years preparing you for adulthood. You'll need a healthy dose of confidence to live a happy and fulfilling life. Here are some examples of where confidence is used in your daily life:

Goal Achievement

What goals do you have that you've pushed to the back of your mind because you don't think you can achieve them? Do you know that you only doubt yourself because you don't have enough confidence? The most successful people in the world got where they are today, not because they're necessarily the most talented or had their parent's financial support, but because they believed in themselves. In fact, for most successful people, the odds were stacked against them but they chose to block out the voices of the naysayers and focus on that little voice within that was saying, "You can do it." That's confidence.

The book Shoe Dog, about Nike founder Phil Knight, is a great example of how confidence and work ethic can be used to push through obstacles and accomplish incredible things. If you need some inspiration, I highly recommend it. Phil Knight went from selling shoes out of the back of his car at track meets to building one of the biggest companies of all time. He had this crazy idea that he could get everyone on earth to wear a pair of his shoes, and his journey to make that happen was just as crazy. Without confidence and the right mindset, he would have never achieved his goal and Nike would not exist.

Socializing

As a teenager, you're always meeting new people. Whether you meet them at a party, a school sports match, or through another friend.

How do you feel, knowing you're about to meet new people? Are you excited or are you worried that they won't like you because of the things you don't like about yourself? We want you to be excited about meeting new people because you get to learn about their life experiences, gain a different perspective and have fun! But when you have low self-confidence, you're too busy focusing on your insecurities to get to know people and allow them to get to know you.

Personal Development

Personal development is about becoming the best version of yourself. To achieve this, you must be able to take a step back and look at your life without bias in order to know what areas need improvement. People with low self-confidence feel uncomfortable evaluating themselves because the process highlights the qualities they don't like about themselves. This can add to their insecurities. However, the main focus of personal development is to work on your strengths so you can become better. Personal development requires confidence, so you don't get caught up focusing on your negative attributes.

Academic Performance

Research suggests that confidence is the number one predictor of academic performance. This is especially true for the main subjects like math, English, and science. Let's face it, school can be challenging, and some students have better experiences than others. You're constantly learning new information, doing assignments and taking tests. Sometimes, it can be very challenging, and getting low grades can make you feel like you need to improve. A person with self-confidence understands that it's okay to get low grades sometimes and that it's okay to find the new subject you're learning difficult.

Healthy Coping Skills

Life is full of ups and downs, and good things will not always come your way. It's important to know this so that you can prepare for it. School is a major source of stress in a teenager's life. Not only are you finding your identity and dealing with peer pressure but your parents and teachers have made it clear that you need good grades to either get to the next academic level, go to college or get a job. Without confidence, you'll find it very difficult to cope with the stresses of life. This is one of the main reasons some teenagers turn to alcohol and illegal drug use. Confidence allows you to develop healthy coping skills to deal with all life's challenges.

WHY SOME TEENAGERS HAVE LOW SELF-CONFIDENCE

Low self-confidence is not a natural state of being; people aren't born this way. There's always something that triggers it. In other words, it might not be your fault that you have low self-confidence. Some of you reading this can think back to the time in your life when you developed low self-confidence. For those of you who can't, here are some reasons why people typically have low self-confidence:

Upbringing

Some parents can unintentionally cause low self-confidence in their children by doing things like comparing them to their siblings, having unrealistic expectations for them, or even spoiling a child to the point where they start to believe they can't do things without someone's help.

Abuse

Unfortunately, not everyone was raised in a safe environment. Some live in abusive households. If you know you were raised in an abusive household, please speak to someone you trust, like a teacher, counselor, or family friend, to get the help you need. Whether emotional or physical abuse, these dramatic experiences can and will destroy a person's self-confidence if not addressed. In most cases, the victim is blameless yet still blames themselves for the abuse, leading them to grow up feeling completely worthless.

Life Experiences

You may have had a perfectly healthy upbringing, but something happened during your childhood that destroyed your confidence. For example, you were picked on in school because your nose was bigger than average, your hair was really curly, you were short, or you didn't have the trendiest clothes. Most children are not looking in the mirror thinking there's something wrong with them; it's other children who point out their so-called "defects," and that's when they become insecure.

Media Influence

As I'm sure you've realized, the media is extremely biased. The people who get the most promotion all look a certain way. You can't help but notice that all the women are slim and pretty with long hair, and all the men are tall with ripped bodies. The more you're exposed to these images, the more you realize that you don't fit what the media promotes as attractive. But what makes it worse is that the people in school who look like celebrities on social media get the most attention and those who don't fit that image get put into a different category.

Anxiety and Depression

Anxiety and depression, although real medical conditions, can often result from focusing on the wrong things. I have overcome these things in my life by changing my perspective and focusing on gratitude. By focusing on what I am grateful for, I can calm my mind and start finding joy.

THINGS GENUINELY CONFIDENT PEOPLE DO DIFFERENTLY

I firmly believe in the saying, "Fake it until you make it," because confidence doesn't develop overnight; it takes practice. But there are some things that genuinely confident people do because it's in their nature. Once you become confident, these things will become a part of your nature too.

They're Not Judgmental

Being judgmental towards others often stems from our insecurities and lack of self-confidence. When we judge others, we essentially project our fears and doubts about ourselves onto them. However, people with healthy self-worth and self-confidence typically have a more accepting and understanding view of others. They see the value that each person brings to the world. Practicing being non-judgmental can lead to a more fulfilling and compassionate life. It can be challenging to break the cycle of judgment, but it is possible. One helpful tip is to practice empathy and try to understand not only where others are coming from but also what they may have walked through to get them where they are today. Remember, everyone has something unique and valuable to offer the world.

They're Happy

Happiness is essential because, to be confident, you must be happy with who you are. Confident people do not rely on other people or circumstances to make them happy. For confident people, confidence comes from within. They invest time and effort into nurturing their emotional well-being, recognizing their strengths and accepting their imperfections. By cultivating a positive relationship with themselves, they lay the foundation for a deep and lasting sense of happiness.

Confident people understand that happiness is a journey, not a destination. They embrace personal growth and continuously strive to improve themselves, bringing them fulfillment and joy. They engage in activities and pursuits that align with their passions and values, allowing them to tap into their innate talents and abilities. By living authentically and pursuing their aspirations, they derive a sense of purpose and happiness from within.

It's important to note that happiness and confidence are mutually reinforcing. When people are genuinely happy with themselves, it boosts their confidence levels. On the other hand, when they exude confidence, it can attract positive experiences and relationships that further contribute to their happiness. This positive feedback loop between happiness and confidence creates an incorruptible cycle that propels personal growth and overall well-being.

They Listen

Listening to others is crucial, especially for confident people who desire continuous improvement. These individuals understand the significance of absorbing information and actively seek opportunities to broaden their knowledge. By being attentive listeners, they open themselves up to a vast array of insights and perspectives.

The importance of listening lies in its profound impact on personal growth and self-improvement. Through attentive listening, confident individuals gain access to many ideas, experiences and viewpoints that they might not have encountered otherwise. Each conversation becomes an opportunity for growth and learning, as they embrace the diverse perspectives shared by others.

Moreover, being a good listener allows confident individuals to build stronger connections with those around them. When people feel genuinely heard and understood, they develop a deeper sense of trust and respect for the listener. This creates an environment of open communication and fosters meaningful relationships.

They Challenge Themselves

Confident people are not afraid to challenge themselves, because they want to improve. They want to sharpen their skills and become the best version of themselves, so they're constantly pushing themselves to do better. They set goals for themselves and take the necessary steps to achieve them. Confident people possess a remarkable trait; they embrace challenges despite fear and without hesitation. They understand that they must continuously push their limits to grow and improve. These people have an unwavering desire to become their best version, which drives them to consistently seek opportunities for self-improvement.

Rather than settling for mediocrity or succumbing to complacency, confident individuals actively pursue avenues that allow them to enhance their skills and abilities. They acknowledge that true growth lies beyond their comfort zone, and they willingly step into the realm of discomfort and uncertainty. By doing so, they expand their horizons and unlock their full potential.

They're Not Attention Seekers

Do you know anyone who always has to be the center of attention? They're really loud and always involved in some type of drama. These people are often mislabelled as confident because of their ability to put themselves out there. The truth is merely the opposite; they're not confident. They are just attention seekers. Because attention seekers have low self-confidence, they're always looking for outside validation to make themselves feel good and do anything to get it. On the other hand, confident people don't seek external validation because they know who they are and don't need anyone to tell them they're awesome.

Are you convinced that confidence is essential? Before you start your journey, it's important to remember that confidence isn't about being perfect; it's about accepting and embracing who you are, including your flaws and imperfections. With confidence as your ally, you can overcome anything that comes your way and live the authentic and fulfilling life you know you deserve.

HERE'S A QUICK RECAP OF WHAT YOU'VE LEARNED IN THIS CHAPTER:

- Self-confidence is about trusting in your abilities, capabilities and judgment. It's a belief that you can successfully meet the demands of the task at hand.
- The main characteristics of self-confidence are self-acceptance, assertiveness, resilience and a growth mindset.
- Teens need self-confidence for goal achievement, socializing, personal development, academic performance and healthy coping skills.
- Some teenagers have low self-confidence because of their upbringing, abuse, life experiences, media influence, anxiety and depression.
- Genuinely confident people do things differently. They're not judgmental. They are happy. They listen, challenge themselves and are not attention seekers.

ACTIVITY: WHAT'S YOUR LEVEL OF SELF-CONFIDENCE

Okay, so now that you're more familiar with what confidence is, it's time to start getting some! The first step to becoming more confident is knowing your confidence level. Here's an activity to help you better understand this.

Below are 10 statements about confidence. Respond to each statement honestly, using the following scale:

- Strongly agree = 4 points
- Agree = 3 points
- Strongly disagree = 2 points
- Disagree = 1 point

Once you've scored all 10 statements, add up your total. The higher your score, the more self-confidence you have. The lower your score, the less self-confidence you have. Be as honest as possible with your responses. There is no right or wrong answer; it is just your current viewpoint. Below is the score chart to measure your final score.

30 – 40 points = High self-confidence

20 – 29 points = Moderate self-confidence

10 – 19 points = Low self-confidence

Let's get started!

10 CONFIDENCE STATEMENTS:

1. I feel confident about who I am as a person.

2. I am comfortable walking into a room of people I don't know.

3. I never compare myself to others regarding looks or achievements.

4. I am confident about the way I look.

5. I am confident about my academic performance.

6. I am confident around people who are doing better than I am.

7. I know what my strengths and weaknesses are.

8. I am confident in my abilities, even when people don't compliment me.

9. Working on myself will help me become more confident.

10. It doesn't bother me when I am not always the best at something.

EVEN IF YOU receive a low score, there's no need to feel discouraged; your confidence can thrive as long as you're willing to put in the effort. Remember, you're like a diamond that requires polishing to radiate its brightest brilliance, and we are here to support you in achieving that!

Now is the perfect moment to translate knowledge into action and embark on the journey of building confidence. In the next chapter, you will discover valuable insights on harnessing the power of your mind and conquering negative thinking patterns.

CHAPTER 2
THE MIND GAME

 Before you can solve a problem, you've got to know what the problem is.

WHEN ASKED WHAT THE MOST POWERFUL WEAPON IN THE WORLD IS, MOST people will say something like a nuclear bomb or some other form of instrument capable of mass destruction. But the truth is, the most powerful weapon in the world is the mind. Every person alive on the planet today has access to the most powerful weapon in the world, including you. Now that's definitely something worth acknowledging. Let me tell you why. It's because everything is first conceived in the mind. The nuclear bomb was designed by an American theoretical physicist named Julius Robert Oppenheimer. Before he saw it physically, he saw it as an idea in his mind. He thought about it and then took action to turn it into reality. In other words, without the mind, there would be no nuclear bomb. So what does this have to do with confidence? Everything! That's where confidence starts. When you don't believe you're good enough, it's because that's what you tell yourself. If you're confident in your mind, your heart can believe you're confident and your actions will reflect that confidence.

HOW TO OVERCOME NEGATIVE THINKING

In this chapter, you will learn how negative thinking affects your confidence and how to overcome it.

What Are Negative Core Beliefs?

One of the realizations I had when writing this book is that the brain is like a computer. Let me explain what I mean by this; I'm sure you own a computer or smartphone, right? The part of the device you can't see is called the hard drive; this is where all the information you've ever entered into the device is stored. Let's say your computer malfunctions and you lose all your work. When you take it to a computer store for repair, they'll first search for your lost work in the hard drive, because that's where it's stored. Your subconscious mind is the hard drive.

Your brain is made up of two parts, the conscious mind and the subconscious mind. Your conscious mind is where you do all your thinking, and the subconscious mind takes in all the information collected by your five senses and files it away. According to experts, by the time you're 18, your subconscious mind will have stored the equivalent of 100 encyclopedias' worth of information! The mind is truly a work of art. The problem is that the subconscious mind doesn't discriminate. It doesn't filter out or reject the bad information; it accepts that information too. Most people assume their life goes in a particular direction because of fate. That's the hand they were dealt, and that's where they are stuck regardless of whether or not it is a good or bad situation. But the truth is that your subconscious mind is like software that programs you to live your life the way you do.

The famous philosopher Aristotle said, "Give me a child until he is 7, and I will show you the man." He meant that everything you learn by age 7 is who you will become as an adult. Why? Because everything you've been exposed to up until that point has become your reality. Your subconscious mind believes that is who you are, and it will steer your life in that direction. For example, if you were raised in a household with no discipline, where your parents woke you up a half-hour before school and rushed around the house getting ready, then that's how you're likely to act as an adult. This is not to say these traits cannot be changed, but overcoming what you learned during childhood will take a conscious effort.

Your negative core beliefs are your beliefs about yourself that are formed by bad past experiences, real or imagined. They are the ideas about yourself that have been instilled in you since birth. They're like the roots of a tree that have been firmly planted in the ground. And now, as a teenager, you've accepted them as facts, and you are acting accordingly. For example, if you were told or shown as a child that you were not good enough in school, you probably internalized this and accepted it about yourself as fact. These internal feelings lead you to not make an effort with your schoolwork because you believe you won't do well anyway, so there's no point in trying. This doesn't sound very encouraging, but before you can solve a problem, you've got to know what the problem is. And the good news is that there is a solution!

HOW NEGATIVE CORE BELIEFS AFFECT TEEN CONFIDENCE

Negative core beliefs can destroy your confidence, because when you believe something is a fact, you won't try to challenge that fact. As far as you're concerned, these beliefs are fixed, and you can do nothing about them. Here are a few ways negative core beliefs can affect your confidence.

Making Friends

When you have a negative view of yourself, also known as self-perception, you doubt your value and self-worth. These feelings appear in social situations and can make you question whether you're likable or interesting. This thought process acts as a barrier to making friends because it stops you from being your authentic self and robs you of your ability to connect with others on a genuine level.

A negative self-perception can also cause you to fear rejection, where you then begin to anticipate the worst and assume that people will reject or judge you. This fear becomes real because you believe it. For example, you're on your way to a friend's birthday party, and you have all these thoughts in your head that people will think you're weird, they won't like you, you're going to embarrass yourself, etc. You literally spend your journey envisioning scenarios where these things happen. By the time you get to the party, you're flustered and anxious, and you end up acting awkward and weird. You try and have a conversation but keep tripping up on your words, or you even get so nervous that you end up falling on your face when participating in something you're normally good at. This is because you worked yourself into a frenzy and invited these things to happen. FEAR is the acronym for False Evidence Appearing Real; the evidence is false because it's something you've imagined. But because you're so focused on it, it seems real.

When you're around people you don't know, instead of engaging in small talk, you'd rather stand on the sidelines and be a silent observer. Why? Because you're scared of saying the wrong thing and being seen as boring or weird.

Jealousy/Envy

Jealousy causes you to constantly compare yourself to others, whether it's the people around you or the people you see on social media. This constant feeling of inadequacy can fuel envy because you desire to have the same things as everyone else.

This feeling of inadequacy makes you worry that you're not good enough to be included. The fear worsens when you see someone else achieving something you want or getting the attention you crave.

You start resenting their success because it highlights what you feel are your failures. Instead of celebrating their accomplishments with them, you feel threatened by them.

Your negative core beliefs affect your confidence because they make you rely on others' affirmation and approval to feel good about yourself. When you don't get this approval, you feel invisible, overlooked and even betrayed by the people closest to you, which can spark jealousy.

Perfectionism

Perfectionism sounds like a good thing, and it can be when it doesn't slow you down. There's absolutely nothing wrong with wanting to do everything with excellence. The problem is that perfectionism can become a hindrance and cause you to not do anything at all. For example, you've been asked to give a presentation in front of your class. Due to your negative core beliefs, you don't think you're good enough to get this right, so you spend weeks preparing for it. But at the last minute, you withdraw because you don't think you've perfected your presentation.

WHY IS NEGATIVE THINKING SO COMMON?

I don't mean to be pessimistic, but if we are being honest, we live in a negative world. It has become the norm to focus on the negative and only talk about our struggles. Have you ever taken the time to listen to what the average person talks about? Suppose you hear your parents talking or overhear a conversation on the bus. Maybe it's about something bad or a story being told in a negative light. It could be a tragedy they've heard about on the news—the rising cost of living expenses, increased crime rates, or others gossiping about someone they don't like. Regardless of the form, negativity is considered normal, so the moment you disrupt that, you may become the odd one in a group of peers. Others might begin to see you as

CHAD & KRISTI METCALF

different because you have a mindset that is foreign to them. People will start accusing you of believing you're better than everyone for refusing to engage in negativity. Unfortunately, these are some things you'll experience as you become more positive. Below are a few main reasons negative thinking is so common:

Media Influence

We live in a world that tells us who we should be instead of being allowed to be who we are. Whether we turn on our TV, log on to social media, or are just talking to a friend, we constantly receive messages telling us we're not good enough. All women are supposed to be slim, with a sharp pointy nose, a big chest, and long, flowing, shiny hair if they want to have any chance of getting a boyfriend and living happily ever after. All men should be six feet tall and above, with a six-pack, a full head of hair, and perfectly clear skin to get a girlfriend and live happily ever after. If you're not wearing the latest designer clothes or going to the cool places teenagers should visit, you're just not good enough. Teenagers aren't the only people affected by these messages; adults are too. So if you don't measure up, and even if you do, you begin to feel as if you're not good enough, and you start telling yourself this.

Personal Experiences

If you've had a lot of negative experiences, you're not going to see the world through a positive lens. We live in a world where people expect instant gratification and where all we see are people's highlight reels. When you compare yourself to others and their highlight reel, you will turn even experiences that should be positive into negative ones, losing your gratitude and confidence along the way.

Ignorance

PEOPLE ASSUME that they can't control their thoughts because it's not something they've been taught how to do. Most people do not even think about the thoughts that go through their head, nor do they stop to analyze them. I know I didn't. I used to believe that controlling my thoughts was beyond my grasp. But life had other plans for me. I'm a real estate agent, and I thrived within my comfort zone, selling homes to people within my sphere of influence. However, I knew there was untapped potential beyond those familiar people.

One day, I decided it was time to break free from my familiar territory and I realized that to grow my business, I needed to confidently approach people I had never met before. It was a daunting challenge for me, as I was not used to stepping out of my comfort zone.

I started my journey towards confidence by immersing myself in communication books and personal development. These books were my compass, guiding me toward self-awareness and mental focus. I began to analyze my own thought process, dissecting my internal dialog like I was unraveling the mysteries of a complex real estate deal.

With time, I grew more self-aware and started to control my thoughts and self-doubt. Armed with newfound confidence, I ventured beyond my comfort zone. I started to approach strangers, strike up conversations out in public, and forge connections. It was a revelation - just like selling a house, I could learn how to direct my own thoughts and the more I did it, the easier it became.

This transformation wasn't just about my career; it was about personal growth. I realized that the key to success in the modern world was not just about what you knew, but also about how confidently you could communicate and connect with others. As a real estate agent, I had to talk to people I'd never met before, and now, I can do it with ease.

My journey taught me that controlling my thoughts and having confidence in myself were essential skills for success. The real estate world, like life itself, is full of opportunities beyond our comfort zones. And I was ready to embrace them with open arms, knowing that my thoughts were no longer holding me back.

HOW TO IDENTIFY NEGATIVE CORE BELIEFS

Identifying your negative core beliefs is the first step to overcoming them. Here are some tips on how to do this.

Reflect on Your Childhood

Try and remember when the negative beliefs started, is there a particular event that caused the negative belief in the first place? I have found that our negative beliefs are often based on something that isn't even true. If we can identify the lies we tell ourselves, we can quickly eliminate these negative beliefs. On the other hand, if the negative belief is based on something true, then that gives us something to work on.

Thought Patterns

Pay attention to your thinking patterns. What do you think about throughout the day? What's going through your mind when you're in social situations? To get a clear picture of this, periodically open up the notes app on your phone and write down your thought patterns for a week straight. At the end of the week, look back on your notes and reflect on what you wrote.

Triggering Situations

Take note of events or situations that bring up strong negative emotions. Ask yourself, "What is it about this situation that makes me feel this way?"

Ask Friends and Family

I understand that asking friends and family members might be difficult because you might not trust people enough to take this step yet. If so, that's totally fine; you can sit this one out. However, your friends and family members pay close attention to you, and they may be able to spot things that you haven't noticed about yourself. Those around you may recognize your gifts and talents before you do. Having someone help you realize your gifts and talents is one of the best ways to eliminate negative core beliefs. This happens because once you know your gifts, you will start focusing on them.

Common examples of negative core beliefs include the following:

- I am a failure.
- I am worthless.
- I can't trust anyone.
- I can't trust my friends.
- People are always laughing at me.

Once you've identified your negative core beliefs, the next step is to work on overcoming them.

OVERCOME NEGATIVE CORE BELIEFS WITH POSITIVE THINKING

Positive thinking, simply put, is about thinking good thoughts, but there's much more to it. Positive thinking is a mindset. It's how you think about yourself and how you view and approach life's challenges with hope and optimism. It's a mindset that says, "Hey, I don't like what I'm going through at the moment, but I know it's temporary and there's a greater purpose for it. Positive thinking is about acknowledging the reality of a situation and choosing to focus on the positive aspects of it. Here's an example from a story I came across while working on this book:

Jessica's story – A 16-year-old girl from Fort Lauderdale, Florida.

"I was raised in foster care. My parents put me up for adoption when I was born. I've never known my birth parents, so it didn't bother me when I was growing up. But because I moved from foster home to foster home, I felt abandoned. I felt as if no one wanted me; why wouldn't anyone adopt me? What made it worse was that I didn't have any friends because I was always moving around so much. I was never at the same school for longer than two years. When I was 13, I turned to drugs and alcohol to block out reality and started running away from my foster homes. It wasn't long before I got arrested and ended up in a juvenile detention center.

While there, I had to attend the 12-step program for alcohol and drugs, and that's when I met Miss Silvia, the lady who conducted the program. She was a wonderful woman who treated me like I was her own daughter. She really helped me to change the way I looked at my situation. The first thing she noticed about me was how good of a writer I was. We had to write mini-essays in class. Miss Silvia quickly recognized that I had a gift for writing, so she encouraged me to keep a journal and write short stories. That was the first time anyone had said anything good about me, and it made me really happy.

Every week, Miss Silvia would talk with me about life and advise me on how to navigate it. But one thing she said that hit home for me was that I needed to take responsibility for my actions. She explained that it wasn't my fault that I hadn't been adopted. It was because the system is complicated and that this happens a lot. But she also said my behavior makes adoption harder because people are scared to take in rebellious children. Suddenly, the lightbulb went on, and from that moment on, I decided to clean up my act and become a girl that people would love to have around. When I got out, I quit drinking and smoking and focused on my schoolwork. I took responsibility for my actions and changed my way of thinking. I went from believing I was worthless and no one would ever adopt me to believing I was worthy of adoption and would become a permanent member of a loving family. Eighteen months after leaving the juvenile detention center, I got adopted, and I've never been happier. My family is fantastic, and I love them with all my heart. I even wrote to Miss Silvia and told her all about it!"

Jessica's story is an inspiration to many people, so I felt it was important to share her story in this book. Her story reminds me how lucky I am to have three amazing sons who love me for who I am and how crucial it is to believe in your dreams if you want them to come true. Positive thinking is so powerful - once you change your mindset, there's nothing you can't achieve.

WHAT POSITIVE THINKING ISN'T

Positive thinking sounds great, but it can also work against you if you're not careful. Positive thinking isn't about pretending your problems don't exist. That's the worst thing you can do. When something comes up, you must deal with it head-on. Don't push things to the back of your mind, and expect positive thinking to resolve them for you. Whatever issues you're having, manage them accordingly. The reality is that you can't always be positive, and doing so is called 'toxic positivity.' Yes, toxic positivity is a real thing! It is when someone excessively and insensitively promotes positive thinking over genuine emotional expression, particularly in situations where individuals may be going through difficult experiences or emotions.

For example, if someone is struggling with grief after losing a loved one, and another person tells them to "just focus on the positive" or "cheer up," this can be an example of toxic positivity. It dismisses the person's genuine emotions and can make them feel like they are not allowed to express their feelings. This can be damaging and unhelpful, as it may prevent the person from processing their emotions and healing in a healthy way.

It's important to remember that, while positive thinking can be helpful in some situations, it is not always the solution and everyone has the right to express their emotions authentically.

THE BENEFITS OF POSITIVE THINKING

 If you spoke to your friends the way you speak to yourself, it's possible you wouldn't have any friends.

Positive thinking isn't just some random theory that someone made up; its benefits are backed by science. Don't worry, I'm not going to get all scientific on you, but it's essential that you understand how positive thinking can change your life for the better.

Less Stress

A little bit of stress is a normal part of life. You get stressed when you've got an exam or need to meet a homework deadline, but that's healthy stress; it ensures you get off your backside and get stuff done. Unhealthy stress is when you're worried all the time. For example, you're constantly worried about your weight, or whether you're good enough or smart enough. You know, the thoughts you might have when you're on your way to school or getting ready to meet a group of friends. The problem with this type of stress is that it damages your body. According to the American Psychological Association, continuous stress can increase the risk of stroke, heart attack and high blood pressure.

Improved Mental Health

I believe your mental health is essentially all your thoughts added up. The more positive your thoughts are, the better your mental health will be. This takes work, so start with the easiest ones and work from there. As you begin to change your thinking from negative to positive, you will build momentum toward confidence and a healthy mind.

Better Relationships

You'll find that people are drawn to your positive vibes, and they'll want to be around you all the time. Your friends and family will want to know about your new state of mind, which will be a perfect opportunity to talk about what you've been learning!

Better Grades

Yes, it's true! Positive thinking can help you get better grades in school. Do you want to know why? When you believe in yourself and approach your work with a positive attitude, you're more likely to try your best, even if you don't like the subject. Negative thinking says, "I'm no good at math, so there's no point in trying." But positive thinking says, "I know I'm not very good at math, but I'm going to do my best and ask my teacher if I need help." Can you see the difference in this approach?

5 WAYS TO PRACTICE POSITIVE THINKING

Remember I said your negative core beliefs were like the roots of a tree firmly planted in the ground? What happens when you cut down a tree and leave the roots intact? The tree grows back. But when the roots are pulled out of the ground, it never grows back. That's what positive thinking does to your negative core beliefs; your new way of thinking and the new things you believe about yourself will uproot those old beliefs, and you'll start flourishing. It's also important to mention that your mindset isn't going to change overnight. Start with the easiest thoughts to change and stack little wins on top of each other, focus on each little step, and before you know it, you'll arrive at your destination!

With that being said, here are three ways to practice positive thinking:

Affirmations

Did you know that affirmations can change your life for the better? It's all about repeating positive statements to yourself every day. At first, it might feel strange, and like you're not being truthful to yourself, but that's normal. The truth is it takes time to fully believe and embrace these affirmations. Keep at it, and eventually, you'll start to see a shift in your mindset and behavior. You got this!

Choose one affirmation a week, write it down on a few Post-it notes, and stick them on your fridge and mirror (these are the two places you're most likely to see them throughout the day). If you're going out, carry your affirmation with you. Say your affirmation ten times out loud when you wake up in the morning and ten times before you go to bed at night. You can also say your affirmation when you catch yourself thinking negative thoughts.

Here are 10 of my favorite affirmations:

1. I am capable of achieving my dreams and goals.
2. I embrace and love myself for who I am, including my strengths and weaknesses.

3. I believe in my abilities and trust that I am capable of making the right decisions.
4. I am responsible for my own happiness and create it for myself.
5. I believe in myself and my potential to make a positive impact on the world.
6. I am capable of handling any challenge that comes my way.
7. I am worthy of love and happiness, and I attract positive relationships into my life.
8. I am resilient and can bounce back from any setbacks.
9. I am kind and compassionate towards myself and others.
10. I am proud of who I am and the person I am becoming.

Affirmations are a good start, but their effect is amplified when we take action on the affirmations we are making. For example, if I say, "I am capable of achieving my dreams and goals," but I just stay on the couch and don't go after my dreams, am I really going to believe it? Probably not! However, if I take action toward my dreams and goals and start making progress, I will start to believe the affirmation more and more. So don't just think it or say it. Start taking action. If you fail at first, which you probably will, don't get discouraged; this is how we learn. We learn how to do things by first learning how not to do them.

Be Kind to Yourself

If you spoke to your friends the way you speak to yourself, it's possible you wouldn't have any friends. The cruel, harsh criticism you give yourself when you're not happy with your performance or the things you say to yourself when you look in the mirror and don't like the reflection staring back at you; can root themselves in your mind. If you would never say these things to a friend, don't say them to yourself. Be more compassionate and kind to yourself by thinking about what you'd say to a friend or a loved one and repeating those words to yourself instead of the cruel, harsh words you're used to.

Get Off Social Media

Most teenagers love social media apps like Snapchat, TikTok, and Instagram. While it has its benefits, such as connecting with friends and finding out the latest news, it can also be extremely harmful when you lack confidence. Social media isn't real life, and anytime you log onto these sites, you're bombarded with images of fake perfection. Celebrities and influencers all showcasing their wonderful lives, bodies, and talents. Exposure to these images leaves you feeling like you're not good enough, which triggers your negative thinking patterns. You can avoid this by not logging onto social media until you become more confident and know how to filter the information and view it through a different lens. The less you're exposed to false images of perfection, the more you will begin to like yourself, and your confidence will grow.

Recondition Your Mind

You developed your negative core beliefs because you've spent your life thinking the same things about yourself over and over again. So, now you have a record player stuck on repeat in your subconscious mind. You can disrupt this narrative by reconditioning your subconscious mind through visualization. This is where you will take the things you have been affirming and start imagining them happening. This doesn't mean you sit around all day daydreaming. It means that when you're facing a challenge, like writing a paper for school or meeting a bunch of new people, you'll visualize a positive outcome and then go for it. While this won't guarantee a perfect outcome, it will give you a much greater chance for success. Visualization is a tool to help you relax and focus; it is a way to defeat the panic and anxiety that comes from self-doubt. Everyone faces feelings of insecurity and self-doubt at some point, so know that you are not alone and that you can recondition your mind.

Scripting

IF YOU'VE EVER BEEN SENT to detention in school, you'll know that one of the punishments is to make you write the same sentence over and over again. Teachers administer this punishment because they understand the power of repetition. When you write something out continuously, you remember it. With that being said, take one of the affirmations listed above and write it out ten times a day for a week. You'll find that by the end of the week, you'll know it by heart, and you'll find yourself randomly repeating it throughout the day.

HERE'S A QUICK RECAP OF WHAT YOU'VE LEARNED IN THIS CHAPTER:

- Your negative core beliefs are the beliefs you've held about yourself since childhood. If you can identify why they started, you can eliminate some of them immediately.
- Your negative core beliefs destroy your confidence and affect your ability to make friends; they cause you to become jealous and a perfectionist.
- Negative thinking is common because of media influence, personal experience and ignorance.
- You identify negative core beliefs by reflecting on your childhood, your thought patterns and triggering situations, and by asking friends and family.
- You can overcome your negative core beliefs through positive thinking.
- Positive thinking is a mindset; it's how you think about yourself, look at life, and approach challenges with hope and optimism.
- Positive thinking isn't about pretending you don't have any problems.
- The benefits of positive thinking are less stress, improved mental health, better relationships, better grades, and increased self-confidence.

- You can practice positive thinking by saying affirmations, being kind to yourself, getting off social media, and reconditioning your mind.

Your mind is a weapon. With the tools you've just learned, you can start using your mind to get the best outcomes in life. In chapter three, you'll learn all about your strengths, how to discover them, and how to use them to really ramp up your confidence.

ACTIVITY: THE REFRAME GAME

Negative thoughts are a reflection of a false reality you've been conditioned to believe. The way you naturally think isn't your fault, but it is your responsibility to challenge yourself and change. This reframe game will help you question your thinking and quickly change your mindset.

Here's how to play it:

1. During the course of one full day, whenever you have a negative thought, write it down on a sheet of paper. At the end of the day, review it and categorize the positive and negative thoughts into two categories, positive and negative. An example of a negative thought would be, "The teacher always calls me out to answer questions in class. He wants to embarrass me because he doesn't like me."
2. Get a sheet of paper and draw a line down the middle of it. On one side of the sheet, write the words: 'NEGATIVE THOUGHT'. On the other side of the sheet, write the words 'POSITIVE THOUGHT.' Transfer your daily thoughts into the two categories. Which one had more? Once you have a list of your negative thoughts, move to step 3.
3. Analyze the thought and decide whether it's a fact or not. For example, it would be a fact if the teacher had said to you that he calls you out to answer questions because he knows you

don't know the answer and wants to embarrass you. However, since the teacher hasn't said this to you, it can't be a fact, because there is no evidence to support it.

4. Since there is no evidence to support the thought, reframe the thought into something more positive such as, "My teacher always calls me out to ask me questions in class because he knows I am capable of answering the questions correctly. He wants me to try harder in my studies." Now this is the important part, take the time to write out the reframed thoughts. Remember writing things down is powerful.

The more you play the reframe game, the better you'll become at reframing your negative thoughts.

CHAPTER 3
UNLEASHING YOUR SUPERPOWERS

 "No one can make you feel inferior without your consent." –
Eleanor Roosevelt

EVERYONE HAS THEIR STRENGTHS AND WEAKNESSES. YES, EVEN YOU. YOU may have hidden your strengths because your peers were less than impressed, and now you don't have the confidence to put them on display. Or you might not know what your strengths are. Either way, knowing and using your strengths is essential to becoming confident. So, in this chapter, we will discuss how to discover your strengths and encourage you to start using them.

HOW TO DISCOVER YOUR STRENGTHS

Whether you're aware of them or not, you've got strengths that make you stand out. But here's the thing, your strengths are more than just being excellent at something. They also have a positive impact on the people around you. The world needs your gifts to make it a brighter and more fulfilling place to live. You may feel a little insecure and uncertain right now, but you'll become more confident and bold once you embrace your strengths and start using them. Let's tap into your strengths and show the world what you're made of.

Strengths – What Are They?

Basically, your strengths are your superpowers. They're the gifts you were born with that make you shine and stand out. These are the things you're naturally good at or that you learn quickly. Many of you will automatically think about school subjects when asked about your strengths because that's what you've been led to believe they are. And that's fine; you can be naturally good at subjects such as math, science, or English/language arts, but these aren't the strengths we are talking about. You may also have some non-academic strengths; tapping into those will also help you learn more about yourself and become more self-confident.

Here are some examples of strengths:

- Creative/singing/dancing/acting/drawing
- Decision making
- Emotional intelligence
- Self-motivated
- Passionate
- Resilient
- Communication
- Writing
- Self-discipline
- Leadership
- Analytical

Why Are Strengths Important?

Your strengths are super important. Unfortunately, many teenagers only focus on the things they're not good at, and that's a bad idea. As mentioned, everyone has their weaknesses, but they're not the things you should pay the most attention to. I'm not saying don't work towards improving in certain areas, but don't obsess about them. Everyone has weaknesses, but the most confident people became confident because they figured out their natural talents and built on them. When you work on something you're good at, you tend to enjoy it more. This has a crazy effect where you actually end up working really hard on it, but it doesn't feel like work because you enjoy it. Sure, there will be times when you don't enjoy it, but is there ever a time you enjoy something you hate doing?

Unfortunately, most people have yet to reach their full potential, because they've never put all their effort into what they're naturally good at. Can you relate to this?

Imagine this, you bring home your report card and get decent grades in every subject but one. Instead of acknowledging the subjects you've excelled in, you only focus on the one class that didn't go well. While some level of this is good, excessively focusing on your weaknesses will lower your confidence and weaken your strengths. A better approach would be to acknowledge what you're doing well, celebrate it, and devise an actionable plan to improve the subject causing you issues.

If you want to reach your full potential, you must know your strengths. Here are some reasons why knowing your strengths leads to a better life:

Boost Your Confidence

You're reading this book to become more confident, right? Knowing your strengths is one way to achieve this. Knowing what you're good at makes you feel accomplished and satisfied. You become self-assured; you believe in your abilities and yourself. You have access to a secret weapon that makes you unstoppable, and that confidence shines through in everything you do.

Authentic Living

When you know who you are, you're not afraid to be yourself. Knowing your strengths is one of the most important aspects of knowing who you are. When you know your strengths, you show up as your authentic self because you've got nothing to prove, and you don't need to pretend to be someone you're not.

Find Your Happy Place

Did you know that the happiest people in the world are those who have found their unique strengths? Several psychological studies have proven this to be true (Seligman, 2004). It makes sense, though. Imagine how it would feel to work on the thing you're naturally good at and enjoy doing every day. You'll jump out of bed with energy and excitement and feel accomplished, self-assured, and capable. When you find the things you're passionate about, your soul comes alive, giving you more determination to achieve your dreams.

I can personally attest to this. After being a Navy SEAL and trying to make the PGA Tour, I didn't know what my strengths were or at least how my strengths applied to the world outside of the military and sports. As a result of this, I lost my confidence for a time. As I started to understand and build my new strengths, I began to build my confidence again. I did this through hard work and learning. I went from 100 job applications and no job to 14 job offers in a year. After several business start-ups, I think I may have found how to use my strengths like the example above. I get out of bed motivated and ready to go, but this was not always the case. I would've laughed at you if you had told me a few years ago that I would be writing books. I actually hated writing growing up, but I just started writing one day. Before I knew it, I'd been sitting there for four hours, completely engaged. I've tried to write every day since. Whether an article, a book, or a script for YouTube, I enjoy the creative process-- especially if it can help someone.

Level Up

Finding your strengths helps you become the best version of yourself. Your strengths are like a compass guiding you on the path towards greatness. When you focus your efforts and energy into the areas you know you're good at, you become more productive, and the more you work at something, the better you'll become at it. Eventually, people will start recognizing you for your talent. Here's a story from a young man I interviewed for this book:

Timothy's Story – A 15-Year-Old Boy From Dallas, Texas

 "I have always loved classical music. My mom said that while she was pregnant with me, I would start leaping in her stomach when she played it. As I grew up, my parents played classical music all the time at home, but I loved the sound of one instrument in particular—the violin. I remember the first time I watched someone play the violin. I was in awe! Her name was Janine Jansen, a tremendous violinist, and I had hoped to play as beautifully as her one day. For my fifth birthday, I asked for a violin, and my parents bought me one. I was so happy. My mom and dad couldn't afford lessons, but I taught myself to play and got pretty good at it.

But I stopped playing the violin when I was 11 because it wasn't considered cool. Everyone was into popular stuff like pop music and skateboarding. I didn't fit in; no one cared about classical music, which made me feel really uncomfortable, so I tucked my violin under my bed and tried to forget it. I started trying to be someone I wasn't so people would like me, but I wasn't happy.

Fast forward two years later, and we had a theater performance at school. I played the part of a street musician who played the violin. I was more than happy to play the role because I was acting. None of my friends would know I really loved playing the violin. I was meant to pretend to play the violin over music. But one day, I went into the gym hall when I thought no one was around to practice my part, and I took my violin out and started playing. Unbeknownst to me, our drama teacher, Mrs. Allen stood at the door and heard me playing. When I finished, she started clapping. I was horrified. My cover had been blown. But Mrs. Allen was so impressed, she asked me to play on the day of the performance. I reluctantly agreed.

That day of the performance changed my life. The joy I felt as I played in front of my school was indescribable. I got a standing ovation, everyone (including the cool kids) was amazed at my talent, and they encouraged me to play more often. My friends called me the 'violinist' from that day on.

After that, I decided to start practicing again. Every day for one hour, I played the violin. I joined a local music club in my town, and it wasn't long before I started playing in competitions and winning. And then people began inviting me to play at their weddings and birthdays. I haven't even finished high school yet, and my music career is taking off like crazy.

I just want to let everyone reading this know that you don't have to be like everyone else. Your strengths make you unique and powerful, and when you find and embrace them, you'll inspire others to do the same".

Timothy exemplifies how tapping into your strengths can transform you from being ordinary to being extraordinary. Some of you might feel that Timothy had a bit of an advantage because he already knew what he was passionate about. You're right; he did. That's why I'm going to help you find your strengths so you can level up just like Timothy.

HOW TO FIND YOUR STRENGTHS

Finding your strengths is a process; some of you might not find them right away, but that's okay. There's no rush; just keep seeking. Here are some tips on how to find your strengths.

Ask Your Family About Your Childhood Passions

During our early years, we find the things that ignite a spark within us. Whether it's doodling on paper, building Legos, or dancing, there was something you were good at when you were a child. Children are explorers. They enjoy trying out different things and dipping their toes into various activities. They have the freedom to pick and choose what appeals to them. As you grow up, these childhood passions evolve and become more refined.

Your parents will know the most about your childhood passions, so start by asking them what you enjoyed when you were little. Once you identify your passions, start working on them again and see if you feel a connection. You might find that you simply grew out of some of the things you were good at, and that's fine. New passions and interests will emerge. It's all part of the adventure of self-discovery.

Think About the Things You Enjoy

What are the things you love doing that make your heart race with excitement, make you lose track of time, and leave you craving for more? The activities that bring you a deep sense of joy are connected to your strengths. You're in your element when you're engaging in the things you enjoy. You're fully present and absorbed in your work because you've connected with your talents and strengths. The things that you enjoy give you insight into your strengths. When you think about the things you enjoy, consider the following:

- What are you naturally drawn to?
- How do you feel when you're engaging in the activity?
- Can you get lost in it for hours?

Pay Attention to the Things People Compliment You On

Sometimes, when you're naturally good at something, you don't really pay attention to it. You almost take it for granted and don't give it a second thought. But your strengths are often the things that people compliment you on and ask you to help them with the most. For example, your friends always compliment you on your style. When they need to shop for a new outfit, they ask you to come along and help them choose what to buy. In this case, you've got an eye for fashion and are good at styling people. Or, you're the person everyone calls when they need advice. In this case, you might have an empathetic gift that makes it easier for you to connect with people on a deeper level.

Become More Self-Aware

Self-awareness is about analyzing your thoughts, feelings, and actions without bias. It's like being able to look in a mirror that reflects your inner world; it gives you insight into what makes you tick and helps you understand yourself on a deeper level. Improving your self-awareness will help you find your strengths because you'll start paying attention to the things that truly light you up inside. You'll develop a stronger attachment to your emotions, which will help you identify patterns in your life. For example, you might notice that you feel more alive and confident when you're expressing your-self creatively, solving puzzles, or leading a group of friends. These emotional cues will point you toward activities that align with your strengths.

HERE ARE **some tips on how to become more self-aware:**

- **Journaling:** Journaling helps you get the stuff in your head out and onto paper. It provides a space for you to release and process your emotions. You can pour out your feelings, frustrations, joys, and everything in between without feeling judged. As you put your experiences into words, you'll gain clarity and a deeper understanding of your emotions.
- **Be Present:** Being present is about living in the moment and paying deliberate attention to the experience you are having. This includes both internally (your thoughts and emotions) and externally (the environment and people around you). Let's say you're at a friend's party, and instead of enjoying the music and the company, you're thinking and worrying about everything you need to get done next week. That's not enjoying the moment. When you find yourself in a situation like that, bring your attention back to the present moment by focusing on something in your environment. If you're having a conversation, tune back into what the person is saying by asking a question related to what they've just said.
- **Self-Reflect:** Teenagers can get so busy hanging out with friends and activities that they don't get a chance to sit and think about what's really going on with their own lives. Self-reflection allows you to hit the pause button, take a deep breath and do some soul-searching. During your time of self-reflection, think about your emotions and why you have these feelings. Think about your relationships with friends and family members and how they're impacting your well-being. You can also reflect on your values, principles, and beliefs and determine how they play a role in your life.
- **Ask For Feedback:** Constructive criticism is powerful because it gives you insight into how other people see you. Friends, family members, teachers, and mentors can help you broaden your self-perception and build resilience. They might point out your weaknesses and tell you things you

don't want to hear, but you can work on self-improvement by embracing constructive criticism with an open mind.

Try New Things

Here's the deal-- you might not have found what you're good at yet because you haven't tried it. Trying new things exposes you to a world of experiences that you may not have discovered otherwise. It forces you to step outside your comfort zone, opening the door to endless possibilities. Whether you try painting, coding, or playing an instrument, each new experience acts as a clue that leads you closer to uncovering your strengths. You might surprise yourself by excelling at something you'd never even considered. Here's the cool part, trying new things isn't just about finding your strengths; it's about expanding your horizons and achieving personal growth. You'll learn essential life skills such as teamwork and resilience, which will all become part of the toolkit you need to confidently navigate the world.

HOW TO USE YOUR STRENGTHS

Practice

Did you know that elite level gymnasts train for 30-40 hours per week and have one day off? Obviously, you've got school, so you can't practice for that long, but my point is that if you want to get better at something, you've got to practice. How long you decide to practice per day is up to you. Just keep in mind the more you work on your skills, the more they will improve.

Volunteering

Volunteering is a great way to use your strengths for the greater good. Not only will volunteering give you a deep sense of fulfillment and purpose, but it's also a chance to make a positive difference and influence the lives of others. Be sure to get permission from your parents first, though.

Make it a Habit

A habit is something you can't stop doing. The idea here is to put your strengths to work every day until they become a habit. For example, if you're good at playing football, styling hair, writing or singing, practice every day until it becomes second nature, meaning you don't need to think about doing it. You just do it.

Finding your strengths is an exciting process of self-discovery. It's a voyage of growth and exploration that will enrich your life in many ways. It's like finding puzzle pieces that fit together perfectly, forming a clear picture of your authentic self. Don't rush the process. Savor every moment and allow yourself to develop a wide range of skills and interests.

HERE'S A QUICK RECAP OF WHAT YOU'VE LEARNED IN THIS CHAPTER:

- Your strengths are your superpowers. They're the gifts you were born with that make you shine and stand out in the world.
- Strengths are important because they boost your confidence and help you live authentically and confidently.
- You can find your strengths by asking your family about your childhood passions, thinking about the things you enjoy, paying attention to what people compliment you on, becoming more self-aware, and trying new things.
- You can use your strengths by practicing, volunteering and making them a habit.

ACTIVITY: STRENGTHS TREASURE HUNT

Finding your strengths is a bit like a treasure hunt because you're searching for something valuable. Even if you think you've found your strengths, I would encourage you to take part in this activity, because you might have other gifts and talents you don't know about. Before getting started, take some time to reflect on your past experiences, both in school and in your personal life. Think about activities, tasks or subjects that have made you feel accomplished or genuinely engaged. Consider moments when you received positive feedback or possibly felt a natural talent shining through.

1. Brainstorm a List of Strengths: Grab a journal or notebook and write a list of 5-10 categories you'd like to explore. These could include leadership, creative pursuits, problem-solving, communication skills, the arts, sports or academic subjects.
2. Decide how long you want to spend on each activity. It could be one day, one week, or one month. It's up to you. However, it's important to remember that some skills will take longer to achieve than others, so plan accordingly.
3. Prioritize the order of operations. Take one category at a time and consume yourself with it for the time you've given yourself. Read books, subscribe to blogs on that subject, and watch YouTube videos from people who have mastered the skill you are trying to achieve.

After completing each activity, write about it in your journal and ask yourself the following questions:

- Did I enjoy anything about this activity?
- Did any talents or skills come up?
- Did I feel excited or a sense of fulfillment while taking part in the activity?
- Did any aspects of the activity feel easy or natural to me?

Once you identify each strength, select one or two strengths from your list and set goals or activities that allow you to further explore and develop those areas. That could involve joining relevant groups or activities, enrolling in related courses, volunteering, or seeking opportunities to apply your strengths in real-life situations.

Remember, this activity is an ongoing process, and strengths can evolve over time. Continually revisit and reassess your strengths as you grow and discover new areas of interest and ability. Once you know what you're good at, your confidence in that area will start growing, and it'll be easier to do away with the things in your life that don't serve you. One of those things is limiting beliefs. In the next chapter, you'll learn what limiting beliefs are and how to crush them for good.

CHAPTER 4
BREAKING FREE FROM LIMITING BELIEFS

 "Don't limit yourself. Many people limit themselves to what they think they can do. You can go as far as your mind lets you. What you believe, you can achieve." ~ Mary Kay Ash

THERE'S AN OLD STORY ABOUT A BABY ELEPHANT WHO WAS TIED TO A fence post. It did everything it could to free itself from the post, but it couldn't. Eventually, the elephant gives up and accepts that it will never escape. The elephant becomes an adult and now has large legs, a massive trunk, and huge tusks. It's bigger than the fence it's tied to and could easily rip itself away. But the elephant has been stuck there for years, and it's accepted that it will remain there forever.

This is how limiting beliefs hinder you. They keep you stuck in a place you've outgrown because you don't believe you're capable of moving any further. If you're feeling stuck at the moment, it could be because you hold limiting beliefs about yourself. In this chapter, we will take a deep dive into what limiting beliefs are and how you can break free from them.

WHAT ARE LIMITING BELIEFS?

Limiting beliefs are the beliefs you hold about yourself that stop you from chasing your dreams. They can prevent you from living a fulfilling life because, deep down, you don't believe you can achieve anything substantial. Instead of striving for your goals, your limiting beliefs will have you doing the bare minimum and scraping the bottom of the barrel.

Our beliefs place limitations and boundaries on what we consider reasonable behavior. For example, most people believe that stealing is wrong, so they won't break into a house and take things that don't belong to them. This example shows that not all limiting beliefs are harmful, our behavior needs boundaries and limitations, otherwise the world would be even more chaotic. They become a problem when your beliefs start to put limitations and boundaries on the behaviors that will help you achieve your goals.

THE THREE TYPES OF LIMITING BELIEFS

Yourself

The limiting beliefs you hold about yourself will hinder you more than anything else. Let's say you have an excellent voice and your dream is to become a singer, but in your mind, you don't have the right look. In fact, you were made fun of in the past about your looks, which has made you even more insecure. Your limiting beliefs will have you focused on your perceived weakness (your looks) instead of your singing talent. As a result, you won't do what's necessary to make your dreams come true, like taking singing lessons or entering competitions.

The World

Your limiting beliefs about the world prevent you from doing things because you're too concerned about what other people will think about you. Do you remember Timothy's story in the previous chapter? Timothy was so concerned with what his friends would think about his passion for playing the violin that he put it under the bed and stopped playing it. That's an example of limiting beliefs about the world. If you're thinking about doing something and your first thought is what will people think, you're already defeated. The reality is that people don't really care as much as you think, because they're too concerned about their own lives to be worried about yours. Also, even if they are against what you're doing, that's their problem, not yours.

Life

Limiting beliefs about life are the ones that force you to give up on something before you've even started. For example, you know you're an excellent writer and come up with an idea for a novel. But something similar has been written before, so you decide you won't bother writing the story. The reality is that there's nothing new under the sun; everything has been done before, but instead of giving up, your job is to do it better!

Your limiting beliefs are not truths; they are false narratives you have convinced yourself are true. Here are some more examples of limiting beliefs:

- I'm not as talented as other people, so there's no point in trying to achieve my dreams.
- I don't deserve success or happiness.
- I'll never have enough money because I don't come from the right family.

- I'm too young to become a speaker. No one will ever take me seriously.
- I'm not attractive enough. No one will ever love me.

HOW DO LIMITING BELIEFS AFFECT YOUR CONFIDENCE?

Limiting beliefs affect your confidence by controlling how you view yourself and your abilities. They create a negative narrative that undermines your self-esteem and prevents you from fully embracing your potential. Here are some ways that limiting beliefs affect your confidence:

Limiting Beliefs Stop You From Pursuing Opportunities

If you don't believe you're good enough, you'll overlook opportunities when they come your way. Let's say you're an excellent cook and everyone tells you they love your cooking. Anytime you have a family dinner, your family tries to get you to make your special lasagna. Anytime a friend has a party, you're always the one they ask to bring a dish. But you have a love--hate relationship with cooking because you have some deep-rooted, unexplainable fear that people won't like your food. So when everyone's eating, instead of enjoying your meal, you monitor their facial reactions with every bite to ensure they're not lying to you. This fear comes from a desperate need to be liked by everyone. If one person doesn't like your cooking, you take it personally and feel they don't like you as opposed to a particular taste. So, when an opportunity to audition for a televised cooking competition comes up, you turn it down because you're afraid of receiving criticism about your culinary skills.

Limiting Beliefs Hinder Your Relationships

Limiting beliefs can keep you from building and maintaining relationships. If you don't believe you're worthy of good friendships, you'll either keep sabotaging them or you won't try to make friends.

For example, you have a new best friend every other week because you keep arguing with your friends, which leads to that friendship ending. Because you haven't identified your limiting beliefs, you don't understand that you're the reason it keeps ending. Think about this, if no matter where you go, you keep experiencing the same challenges and the common denominator is you, there might be something you're doing that needs to change. A limiting belief might make you conclude that people are mean since you can't get along with anyone, so there's no point in trying to make friends.

Limiting Beliefs Give You a Scarcity Mindset

A scarcity mindset is a fear-based way of thinking that makes you believe you'll never be good enough. This fear causes you to make bad decisions that result in negative outcomes. These adverse outcomes confirm your negative thinking, and the cycle continues. For example, you're not great at math and can't see yourself ever getting better at it. So, instead of taking extra classes and getting the help you need, you do nothing and fail your exams. Now you really believe you're no good at math and that you'll never get a decent grade! But the reality is that you didn't try, and you'll never know if you could've passed your exams if you'd have just put in more effort.

HOW TO IDENTIFY LIMITING BELIEFS

WHEN YOU'RE SICK, the best thing to do is go to the doctor and get a proper diagnosis. There's no point in trying to cure yourself by taking a bunch of different medications if you don't know what's wrong with you. The same is true for your limiting beliefs. You need to know precisely what they are before you can overcome them. Here are some tips on how to identify your limiting beliefs.

Journaling

Often, limiting beliefs show up as thoughts. Most people don't say them out loud. One of the reasons you're not aware of them is because they come and go. If you never take the time to reflect on why you think the way you do, you will continue to allow your thoughts to consume and control you. But when you get your thoughts out of your head and onto paper, you can evaluate them and determine whether they're true or not. Once you become aware of your limiting beliefs, you can stop them so they no longer hinder your life. As an added benefit, writing your thoughts down can help relieve stress associated with those beliefs. If you're not sure how to go about journaling to identify your limiting beliefs, here are some prompts to get you started:

- Write down one limiting belief and why you feel it's a limiting belief in your life.
- How often do you think about this limiting belief?
- How does this limiting belief affect your emotions?
- In what way does this limiting belief hinder your progress?
- What could you have achieved by now if you didn't have this limiting belief?
- Where do you think this limiting belief comes from?

Evaluate Your Behavior

Another way to identify your limiting beliefs is to evaluate your behavior. Think about situations where you've acted negatively. If you consider your negative behaviors, you may find that the underlying cause is your limiting beliefs. For example, let's say you're always critical of your friends when they achieve something. Your limiting belief might be that you don't feel good enough to try and achieve what they have accomplished. So, the only way to make yourself feel better is to try and drag your friends down to your level by criticizing them.

Challenging Areas

Where you feel challenged will help you identify your limiting beliefs. Perhaps you have a bad habit of spending all your pocket money on junk food and eating out. A challenge like this could indicate that you don't value yourself enough to care for your health. Write down each challenge and the limiting belief connected to it.

HOW TO OVERCOME LIMITING BELIEFS

Now that you've identified your limiting beliefs, the next step is to work on overcoming them. Here are some tips:

Journaling

Get your journal out again and really start digging into your limiting beliefs so that you can work on overcoming them. Here are a few prompts to consider.

- Is there any evidence to prove your limiting belief is true? Is this limiting belief a fact, or are you jumping to conclusions? Suppose you feel there is evidence to confirm your limiting belief. Does this mean you should continue having this limiting belief, or can you accept that it's possible to change? Just because your feelings are valid doesn't mean they're facts.
- How would your life change for the better if you let go of this limiting belief?
- What action can you take to prove this limiting belief is wrong? For example, if your limiting belief is that you don't think you're good enough to be on the soccer team, you can start training to prepare yourself to try out for the soccer team next year.
- Write down three positive affirmations to replace this limiting belief. If your limiting belief is, "I'll never be good enough to get on the soccer team," one positive affirmation could be, "I am more than capable of becoming a part of the soccer team."

Adopt New Behaviors

Adopting new behaviors and taking action is essential for personal growth and self-improvement. It involves consciously changing certain aspects of your behavior, habits and mindset, to achieve a desired outcome.

Let's say you want to become more organized. Start by researching tools and techniques that will help you achieve this goal and begin implementing them. Being organized can have numerous benefits, such as increased productivity, reduced stress, and better time management. To embark on this journey, follow these six steps:

1. Set Clear Goals: Determine what being organized means and how it will enhance your life. Establish specific and measurable goals that you can strive for.
2. Research Tools and Techniques: Look for tools, strategies and techniques that can assist you in becoming more organized. Various resources, such as books, online articles, apps and videos, can provide valuable insight and practical tips.
3. Declutter and organize: Start by decluttering your physical and digital spaces. Remove unnecessary items, organize your belongings, and create systems to maintain order. This could involve sorting clothes into bins, setting up folders for your schoolwork, using labels, or investing in storage solutions.
4. Develop Routines and Habits: Consistency is key to maintaining organization. Establish daily or weekly routines that support your organizational goals. For example, review your to-do list every morning or tidy up your workspace before finishing work each day.
5. Seek Support from Others: Share your goals with trusted friends and family members who can help hold you accountable and check in on your progress.
6. Monitor Progress and Adjust: Regularly evaluate your progress to determine what is working and what needs adjustment. Be flexible and open to modifying your strategies as you gain more insight and experience.

Remember, adopting new behaviors takes time and effort. Be patient with yourself and celebrate small victories along the way. With consistent action and a proactive mindset, you can gradually develop and maintain the desired behaviors, ultimately achieving your goal of becoming more organized.

Make small changes over time and keep practicing. This will eventually lead to significant changes in your thought process and behavior. It's important to remember that making these changes will take time and patience. It will be challenging at first because your brain is used to doing the opposite. But if you keep practicing, your new behaviors will become the norm, and it won't be so hard anymore.

Adopt a Growth Mindset

In Chapter 1, we discussed what it means to have a growth mindset. In short, it means you believe your intelligence, talents and abilities can be improved and developed through dedication, effort and a willingness to learn. One of the reasons your limiting beliefs keep you stuck is that you don't think there's any point in trying to improve your life. One way to change this way of thinking is through a growth mindset. Here are three tips on how to change your mindset:

Read Stories

There are so many rags-to-riches stories about ordinary people who have done extraordinary things with their lives because they decided they wanted more out of life. They're not people who were born with money and given a head start in life; they came from poor backgrounds, and the odds were stacked against them. Still, they found the strength to escape poverty and become who they are today. A few people whose stories have inspired me include:

Phil Knight, the co-founder of Nike, went from selling shoes out of his car to building one of the world's most iconic and successful athletic brands.

Elon Musk: Born in South Africa, Elon Musk is known for his entrepreneurial spirit and innovation. He co-founded companies like Paypal, Tesla, SpaceX, and Neuralink, revolutionizing the electric vehicle and space industries. He left home at 17 with $2000 in his pocket and worked at a farm, cut logs, worked in a boiler room and various other places before he made it big.

J.K. Rowling: Rowling went from being a single mother on welfare to becoming one of the world's most successful authors. Her Harry Potter book series has captivated readers of all ages and inspired a global phenomenon.

Start with reading these success stories by simply Googling their stories, or you can purchase books about their lives to gain a deeper understanding. Trust me, they will motivate you to ditch your limiting beliefs and start working on fulfilling all of your dreams.

Start Small

By starting small, you won't overwhelm yourself and give up. Whatever areas you're struggling in, give yourself small challenges to improve. If you're overweight and don't see the point in working out because you'll never be as small as your peers, set a goal of cutting out one unhealthy food item from your diet and going for a 10-minute brisk walk daily. Do this for 30 days, increasing the walking time as you go, and see how much weight you lose. Before getting started, weigh yourself and then stay off the scale until the 30 days are up. On day 30, weigh yourself again. Even if you only lost two pounds during the month, how do you feel overall? Did the small amount of effort you put in help you lose some weight and encourage you to keep working on it?

Learn Something New

Get used to challenging yourself by learning something new. You could learn a new language, an instrument, or an academic subject such as economics. Learning something new will force you to step out of your comfort zone and teach you that you can become good at anything if you put your mind to it.

It's important to remember that overcoming your limiting beliefs will take a lot of hard work and patience. But the more you practice, the easier it will become. Instead of focusing on the end goal, examine your progress toward that goal; this will help encourage you to stay on the path.

HERE'S A QUICK RECAP OF WHAT YOU'VE LEARNED IN THIS CHAPTER:

- Limiting beliefs are the beliefs you hold about yourself that stop you from chasing your dreams.
- There are three types of limiting beliefs—the beliefs you hold about yourself, the world, and life.
- Limiting beliefs affect your confidence because they stop you from pursuing opportunities, hinder your relationships, and give you a scarcity mindset.
- You identify limiting beliefs through journaling, evaluating your behavior, and identifying the challenging areas in your life.
- You can overcome your limiting beliefs through journaling, adopting new behaviors, and adopting a growth mindset.

ACTIVITY: S.M.A.R.T GOALS

To get you started on your journey to overcoming limiting beliefs, I want you to set a goal for something you never thought you'd be able to do. The thing that you're most insecure about, whatever that may look like for you. Maybe it's speaking in front of a group, writing a book, or starting acting classes. Whatever your fear is, I want you to attack it with full force using the S.M.A.R.T. goals strategy. S.M.A.R.T. stands for the following words: Specific, measurable, attainable, relevant, and time-bound.

1. Specific – Choose a well-defined and precise goal. Instead of setting a vague goal like saying, "I want to get better grades in math," you should say, "I want to raise my math grades from a C to a B by the end of the year."
2. Measurable – You should be able to measure your goals and track your progress, to determine whether you're likely to succeed. Using the above example, your measuring criteria might be to achieve 80 percent or higher on your tests.
3. Achievable - Your goals should be challenging but realistic. They should get you out of your comfort zone but not be so overwhelming that you become discouraged. For example, setting a goal that you're going to gain more confidence so you can give a presentation in front of 500 people in one month might not be possible. But setting a goal that you will have two conversations per week with people you don't know is more likely to happen. You can build on it from there and make your next goal more difficult.
4. Relevant – Your goals should be something you're passionate about and interested in. Don't follow the crowd, and don't take up a goal because that's what your best friend wants to do. Come up with something that is unique to your dreams for your life.
5. Time-Bound – Goals should have a specific deadline. This helps set a target to work towards and creates a sense of urgency. For example, setting a goal to read three books about effective communication skills in three months gives you a clear timeline.

Unfortunately, not many teenagers chase their dreams because; A) That's not what most adolescents think about; and B) these are not skills taught in most schools. However, I believe you're reading this book because you're different, you want more out of life, and deep down, you want to embrace your uniqueness to become that bright and shining star you know you're capable of becoming. In the next chapter, you'll learn exactly how to do this.

UNLOCK THE POTENTIAL OF TOMORROW'S LEADERS!

 "Confidence is silent, insecurities are loud." - Anonymous

Empowering teens with confidence is a gift that keeps on giving. As you delve into the pages of "Teen Confidence Unlocked," we hope you're inspired and enlightened by what you find. And now, we have a small favor to ask: **Would you be willing to inspire a teen you've never met without spending a dime or seeking any recognition?**

If you're nodding in agreement, we have a heartfelt request on behalf of a young teen you might have never met and even the teens that you do know.

They might be just like you were during your teenage years: full of dreams, seeking affirmation, and looking for a light to guide them into their next phase of life. This is where your words can make a difference.

To further our mission of boosting the confidence of young adults, **we need your voice**. Since many judge books by their covers (and reviews), we humbly request you to spare a minute to post an honest review. It's a small gesture that can have a profound impact.

Your review has the potential to:

- Encourage a teen to believe in themselves.
- Help young students find their true potential.
- Allow someone to embark on a journey of self-discovery.
- Transform countless lives in ways you can't even imagine.
- Light up someone's world with a new vision for their future.

ALL IT TAKES IS a minute of your time to leave a review.

P.S. If you're passionate about uplifting the next generation, you're exactly the kind of reader we cherish. Stay tuned for more empowering content in the subsequent chapters. If for some reason, something has changed and the QR code doesn't work, just leave the review wherever you purchased the book on the product page.

P.P.S. Remember: Lighting someone's path makes you their guiding star. Share "Teen Confidence Unlocked" with other young minds and be a part of their journey.

WITH IMMENSE GRATITUDE,

Chad and Kristi Metcalf

CHAPTER 5
EMBRACE YOUR UNIQUENESS

 "Fitting in allows you to blend in with everyone else, but being different allows you to be yourself, to be unique, and to be more creative." Sonya Parker

ONE OF THE REASONS TEENAGERS TRY SO HARD TO FIT IN IS BECAUSE THEY want to be like everyone else, to be popular, and for everyone to like them. But the reality is that no matter how great you are, there will always be someone who doesn't like you, and that's okay. You'll never become who you were destined to be if you're constantly trying to be someone you're not. Self-acceptance isn't about being perfect. It's about knowing who you are and accepting your perfectly imperfect self. That includes all the insecurities, quirks, and unique qualities that make you who you are. Join me as we challenge these false narratives of perfection and discover the resiliency and strength within you.

WHAT IS SELF-ACCEPTANCE?

Self-acceptance is about being true to yourself and embracing every part of who you are so that you're not hiding behind a mask or pretending to be someone you're not. Self-acceptance gives you the freedom to express yourself honestly and legitimately, without fear of judgment or rejection from others. It means acknowledging your strengths, abilities and unique talents, and being proud of them. And at the same time, it means accepting your limitations and the challenges that you face. Self-acceptance teaches you to embrace your strengths and work on improving your weaknesses without being harsh on yourself. Furthermore, self-acceptance is about accepting that you're a work in progress and that you've still got plenty of growing to do.

While growing, you must step out of your comfort zone, take smart risks, and explore new opportunities. All these will help you become a well-rounded and balanced individual with all the tools required to excel in life. I interviewed a young lady named Jordan about her journey to self acceptance. This is her story:

Jordan's Story – A 18 Year Old Girl From Chicago, Illinois

"Hey, I'm Jordan! I wanted to share something with you all. Being shy doesn't mean there's anything wrong with you! I've always had a soft-spoken voice, and I do not like being in the spotlight. When I was growing up, my parents thought it would help if they sent me to confidence classes (yep, those actually exist). When I was little, I used to run and hide whenever someone came over, because I felt uncomfortable around people. Everyone knew me as "the shy girl," and since it was such a big deal to everyone, I started believing something was wrong with me. I thought I needed fixing, which only made me withdraw even more.

In 5th grade, things got even more challenging when the other kids started being mean. They always asked me why I was so quiet or such a bore. It was really hard for me, and I dreaded going to school every day. But then, when I started middle school, everything changed. I found some amazing friends who were just as shy as me. We had so much in common, like our love for dance, reading and drawing. We would hang out on weekends and have the best time together. Sure, we were considered the "weird kids" by some, but we didn't care because we had each other.

One week, we decided to read this book called <u>The One Week Job Project</u>, by Sean Aiken. (I won't spoil it for you; you should read it yourself!) Inspired by the author's bravery and determination, we came up with a bold idea. We invited our entire class to our national dance competition. I mustered up the courage to ask our teacher if I could put up a notice in the classroom. And guess what? I even stood up in front of everyone and personally invited them to come. To my surprise, a lot of people showed up! I won first place in the competition, and my friend Lizy grabbed second place. I was beyond thrilled about winning, because I had practiced so hard. After the competition, everyone from my class went out for burgers and shakes. I had an incredible time that night and it's one of my favorite memories.

By inviting people into my world who I wouldn't typically hang out with, we all discovered that there was absolutely nothing wrong with being different. Some kids even told me, who I thought disliked me, that they admired me for being unafraid to be myself. So, here's my message to all of you. Don't be afraid to be yourself! It's totally cool to be different. Trust me, you become so much more inspiring when you choose to stand out instead of trying to fit in.

Jordan's story is another breath of fresh air as it highlights the importance of being true to who you are. At the beginning of the chapter, I mentioned that teenagers want to fit in because they're scared people won't like them. But as you've just read, the thing that makes you different is actually what makes you more likable.

WHY IS SELF-ACCEPTANCE IMPORTANT?

Self-acceptance is necessary because it allows you to embrace and celebrate your authentic self.

Here are some of the main reasons why self-acceptance is essential:

Freedom from Comparison

During your teenage years, getting caught up in the comparison trap is easy because you're still discovering who you are. Whether it's your talents, looks or achievements, you constantly compare yourself to others around you. According to the experts, it's normal for teens to compare themselves to each other; it's called "the theory of social comparison." This process helps adolescents discover where they stand regarding preferences, attitudes, and beliefs. Social comparison can motivate and inspire teens. However, there's also a downside to comparison. It can make you feel like your accomplishments are not enough, which can have a negative effect on your self-esteem and lead to envy, guilt and regret. Self-acceptance frees you from the comparison trap, because you understand that everyone is unique and that we all have gifts and talents the world needs.

Authentic Relationships

Have you ever made friends with people because you thought they were really cool and were into the same things as you? You hung around them for a while, but then the cracks started to show. You soon realized they weren't who you thought they were, and if you'd known this from the beginning, you would've never made friends with them. Well, this happens when you don't accept yourself; you become a people-pleaser and a chameleon, and your character and personality change depending on who's hanging around. When people don't know who you really are, they can't make a genuine connection with you. Self-acceptance is necessary if you want honest, authentic relationships with people who accept you for who you are.

Mental Well-Being

Trust me when I say that pretending to be someone you're not and constantly worrying about what others think can be incredibly stressful. It affects your mental health, making you feel anxious and paranoid. You start questioning if people can see through your mask, fearing that you'll be exposed as a fraud one day.

But here's the thing; accepting yourself unconditionally is a game-changer. When you embrace who you truly are, you no longer have to strive for perfection or seek validation from external sources. It liberates you from the heavy burden of trying to meet unrealistic societal standards. You can finally let go of the constant worry about what others think and focus on your growth and happiness instead.

Accepting and valuing yourself opens the door to prioritizing self-care practices that support your overall well-being. Taking care of yourself physically and emotionally becomes a priority. You realize you deserve love, kindness and compassion like anyone else. Engaging in activities that bring you joy, finding healthy outlets for stress, and nourishing your mind and body become vital parts of your journey.

Remember, you were created to be unique and special in your own way. Embrace your authentic self, free from social pressure. Surround yourself with people who appreciate and support you for who you are. Don't let the fear of judgment keep you from pursuing your dreams and living a fulfilling life.

HOW TO ACCEPT YOURSELF

Accepting yourself is an exciting but challenging task. It leaves a bittersweet taste in your mouth because, on the one hand, you can appreciate how liberating it is. But on the other hand, you're scared to death of the transition you're about to make. Nevertheless, I can assure you that you won't regret it. Here are some tips on how to accept yourself:

Practice Self-Reflection

Getting to know yourself is a vital part of self-acceptance. One way to achieve this is through the practice of self-reflection. This involves embracing all aspects of your identity, including your strengths, weaknesses and aspirations.

You can practice self-reflection by doing the following:

Make Time

Self reflection is most effective when you're intentional about it. Therefore, set aside time once a week to engage in this activity. Find a quiet, peaceful place to be alone with your thoughts.

Use your journal for this! Ask yourself meaningful questions, such as:

- What are my interests and passions?
- What are my strengths?
- What are my weaknesses?
- What goals do I hope to achieve?
- What values are important to me?
- Where do I see myself in five years?
- What experiences have shaped me?
- How do I handle setbacks and challenges?
- What brings me fulfillment and joy?

Reflect on Mistakes

Think about some of your biggest mistakes and how they've affected you. Most people don't like making mistakes because it doesn't feel good when you mess up. Still, your mistakes can become powerful lessons if you learn to change your perspective. When you think about your mistakes, consider how they've benefited you. What did you learn from them that made you better or will at least help prevent you from repeating the same mistake?

Embrace Change and Growth

As you reflect, recognize that change is a natural part of life. Embrace the growth that comes with self-reflection. Acknowledge that your thoughts, beliefs and aspirations will evolve over time. Embracing change allows you to adapt, learn and take hold of new opportunities that align with your growing sense of self.

Seek Input

Self-reflection doesn't mean you must embrace the journey alone. You can also seek different perspectives from trusted friends, family members or mentors. They can provide valuable insights, challenge your assumptions and provide support as you navigate your reflections. Consider each opinion; however, don't get too caught up in what everyone else has to say. Use others' voices as a guide.

Take Action

Self-reflection isn't just thinking about your life; it's also about taking action. Use the insights from self-reflection to make positive changes, whether pursuing new interests or working towards your personal goals. Take intentional steps that align with the things you learn about yourself during times of self-reflection.

Embrace Individuality

Did you know that there is no one else on the planet like you? You were born for a specific purpose--to do something on earth that no one else can do. No one else has your fingerprints or DNA. You might have siblings that look like you and friends that act like you, but there is only ONE you. You're a bright and shining star with unique gifts, talents and abilities, and that's something you should celebrate.

Self-acceptance should never be mistaken for complacency. It's essential to recognize that certain aspects of your life are within your control, and some are not. I firmly believe in embracing and loving the person you are, even as you strive to make positive changes. However, if you find yourself feeling insecure about your physical appearance, it's perfectly okay to take steps to address it. Even without a gym membership, alternatives such as jogging or following free workout videos on platforms like YouTube are available.

One of the first steps towards improving your self image is recognizing that the standards pushed by the media are unrealistic. The photographs of celebrities, models and influencers are all edited to make them look perfect, but none look like that in real life. Most of them are regular-looking people with expert stylists and photographers who make them look way more attractive than they actually are. For most people, regardless of fame or status, social media posts are just a small snapshot in time...a highlight reel of their lives. They don't show the bad days, and trust me, we all have bad days. That's why the media makes such a big deal when celebrities are caught off guard and photographed with no makeup. I'm not telling you to ignore your appearance. Just don't beat yourself up for not meeting celebrity standards.

Prioritize your overall health and well-being instead of focusing on perfection. Exercise regularly, nourish your body with healthy foods, and get enough sleep. By focusing on how you feel instead of what you look like, you'll start feeling better about your body.

It's important to practice Self-Care, treat yourself with kindness, respect and compassion. Incorporate activities that help you relax and unwind, such as taking a hot shower, listening to calming music, practicing aromatherapy, journaling, or indulging in a hobby that brings you peace. Spend time with supportive, positive friends. By prioritizing self-care, you cultivate a positive self-image and strengthen your connection with your body.

Take some time to read about body image and self-esteem. The more you learn about the subject, the easier it will be to improve your body image. Read books, listen to podcasts, and speak to other people who are more knowledgeable than you. Understanding the things that contribute to negative body image can empower you to challenge and redefine the unrealistic standards imposed upon us.

Foster and maintain relationships with people who uplift and support you. Spend quality time with friends, family or loved ones, whether it's through shared activities, heartfelt conversations or simply enjoying each other's company. Don't hesitate to reach out for support when you need it. Whether talking to a trusted friend or family member, seeking professional help from a therapist or counselor, or joining support groups, remember that you don't have to face challenges alone.

Remember, some aspects of life are beyond your control, so it's important to avoid wasting time and energy trying to change unpredictable circumstances. The more you strive to control every aspect of your life, the more overwhelmed and anxious you may become. For instance, you can't control people's opinions of you, no matter how kind and genuine you are. Instead of constantly seeking validation or obsessing over why someone may not like you, what should you do? Do you have to be even nicer, plead for their approval, or lose sleep trying to figure it out? Without a doubt, the answer is no. Carry on living your best life, and concentrate on the areas where you hold the power to make a positive impact.

Practicing self-compassion is a great way to cultivate acceptance, understanding and kindness towards yourself. Do you show compassion to your friends, family members and loved ones? When they come to you with a problem, do you insult them and tell them to get over it? No, you comfort them and speak words of kindness to them. So why are we so unkind to ourselves? It's important to understand that the most influential voice in your life is your own because it's the one you hear the most. In a world where people often worry about what others think, it's crucial to prioritize how you speak to yourself, because those internal messages shape your self-perception.

HERE ARE SOME TIPS ON HOW TO PRACTICE SELF-COMPASSION:

- **Mindful Awareness:** Start by becoming aware of your inner voice. Pay attention to how you speak to yourself. What are you saying? Notice when you're being judgmental or self-critical. Mindfulness allows you to observe these thoughts without judgment, creating space for self-compassion.
- **Speak With Kindness:** Replace self-criticism with gentle and kind self-talk. Speak to yourself as you would speak to a friend or a loved one. Offer words of support, understanding, and encouragement. Remind yourself that you're doing your best, and understand that it's okay to make mistakes sometimes.
- **Self-Care:** Prioritize self-care activities that improve your motivation and allow you to recharge. This can include relaxing through deep breathing exercises and meditation, spending time in nature, eating the right foods, getting enough sleep, or engaging in hobbies.
- **Embrace Imperfections**: As I've already mentioned, there's no such thing as perfection. People are so insecure because the media is constantly bombarding us with filtered images of perfection, and we're left feeling like we can't measure up. But I want to remind you that you're fine just the way you are. If you speak with a lisp, embrace it. Maybe you have a gap in your teeth; embrace it. If you're taller or shorter than average, embrace it. Whatever you perceive as an imperfection about yourself, start wearing it with pride.

- **Validate Your Emotions:** Sometimes, we hide our emotions because we don't want to appear weak or burden anyone. Emotions are an essential part of the human experience; they make us who we are and are nothing to be ashamed of. Don't suppress your emotions. Feel and express them in healthy ways, such as by talking to a trusted friend or family member, journaling, or seeking professional help if you need to.

- **Practice Forgiveness:** In the same way you've forgiven others who have wronged you, extend the same forgiveness to yourself. If you've been horrible to yourself, said unkind words to yourself, and diminished your self-confidence, it's time to forgive yourself and start fresh. You're an amazing person with great potential, and that's how you should see yourself from now on. Leave your old way of thinking in the past and embrace your new positive mindset.

And finally, practice, practice, practice! Learning is great, but what use is the knowledge you acquire if you don't apply it to your life? Self-acceptance is one of the most challenging things you'll ever do, because strangely enough, it's easier to wallow in self-pity and focus on your insecurities. It takes hard work and commitment to become a better person. The key is consistency; if you do one thing every day to work towards improving yourself, you'll be a completely different person by the end of the year.

HERE'S A QUICK RECAP OF EVERYTHING YOU'VE JUST LEARNED:

- Self-acceptance is about being true to yourself and embracing every part of who you are so that you're not hiding behind a mask or pretending to be someone you're not.

- Self-acceptance is necessary because it frees you from the comparison trap, allows you to have genuine relationships, and improves your mental well-being.

- You can learn to accept yourself by practicing self-reflection, embracing your individuality, improving your body image, letting go of your desire to control every aspect of your life, and practicing self-compassion.

As you continue the journey of becoming an adult, one crucial aspect is embracing accountability for your actions. Shifting away from playing the blame game is a transformative step, and you will find that life opens up when you wholeheartedly accept responsibility for your mistakes, learn from them and move forward. In the next chapter, we'll dive into some key lessons on embracing accountability and discovering practical strategies for taking ownership of your actions. Get ready to embark on a path of personal growth and empowerment as you learn how to navigate life with integrity and resilience.

ACTIVITY: GRATITUDE JAR

Gratitude is a powerful practice that helps us shift our perspective from focusing on what's wrong with our lives to appreciating the blessings in our lives. Teenagers face a lot of pressure, and it can be difficult to feel content with where you are in life. In this chapter, you've learned about self-acceptance, and one way to help you achieve this is through the daily practice of gratitude.

Materials:

- A jar or other container large enough to hold
- Sticky notes or small strips of paper
- Markers or pens

Instructions:

Step 1: Gather all materials and lay them out on a surface, make sure they are out of the way but somewhere you will see everyday. Next, pick a time of day to visit this spot every day for a month. For example, first thing in the morning when you wake up, after school or before bed.

Step 2: Reflect on one thing you're grateful for every day. It could be family, friends, or a situation that happened.

Step 3: Write down the thing that you're grateful for on your strip of paper.

Step 4: Hold the strip of paper in your hands, read it out loud, and take a moment to think about why you are grateful for it.

Step 5: Now, put the slip of paper in the jar and go about your day.

Step 6: When you're not feeling great, open your gratitude jar, read all your gratitude strips, and remember the things you're grateful for.

CHAPTER 6
OWN YOUR STORY

❝❝ *"It's not only what we do, but also what we do not do, for which we are accountable." ~ Moliere*

PERSONAL ACCOUNTABILITY, THE WILLINGNESS TO TAKE OWNERSHIP OF our decisions, actions and their consequences, is essential to developing self-confidence. Some teenagers shy away from personal accountability because it involves owning up to their mistakes. They think that by admitting failure, they won't fit in and be accepted by their peers. However, the pressure to maintain an illusion of perfection can harm your mental and emotional well-being. When you practice personal accountability, you free yourself from this burden and become the author of your destiny. It gives you the power to write your life story exactly how you want it written because you've chosen to own your decisions and actions. In this chapter, we will explore how mistakes and owning your story are stepping stones toward personal development.

WHAT IS ACCOUNTABILITY?

In her 2019 TEDx talk, 17-year-old Janyssa Berrios perfectly explained accountability. She asked the audience whether they ever feel like bad things always happen to them and that they're never on the receiving end of good news, good health or good fortune. She then asked whether the possible cause of at least some of their distress could be their perspective. Janyssa was bullied all throughout 8th grade, and she hated the girl who caused her so much hardship. One day, after being confronted by the bully, she acted impulsively and ended up in detention, giving her plenty of time to think about the consequences of her actions. While bullying is unacceptable, there are better ways to resolve the issue. Janyssa had to accept that her response to the other student landed her in the trouble she was in. She took accountability for her behavior and concluded that she couldn't control how people treated her but could control how she reacted.

There are several components to personal accountability, which include the following:

- **Taking Responsibility:** Taking responsibility means acknowledging and accepting the consequences of your actions. It involves understanding that your decisions have an impact on your life and the lives of others. In order to take responsibility, you must also think before you act and evaluate the possible outcomes before making a decision. It also includes being humble enough to apologize to the people you hurt, asking for forgiveness when you make a mistake, and doing what's required to make amends.
- **Be Proactive:** Proactive people don't wait for instructions; they step up and take the initiative to get stuff done. Proactivity is about thinking ahead and preparing for future obstacles, to avoid being caught off guard. Proactive people are problem-solving ninjas; they look for solutions and

execute them. They are always ready to take on the next challenge.

- **Being Honest:** Accountability is about being truthful with ourselves and others. It means having integrity even when life gets challenging. Recently, 17-year-old Adrian Rodriguez found a green handbag in a parking lot in Chula Vista, California. It contained $55 and a wallet full of credit cards. Adrian had two choices: keep the bag and its contents or return it to the owner. He chose the latter and took the bag to the address on the driver's license. The lady's name was Melina Marquez; she wasn't home when he returned the bag to her house and had left it with her roommate. But she posted a picture from her Ring camera to find Adrian and thank him. Adrian got more than a thank you. Hundreds of people, touched by his honesty, gifted him with almost $17,000! When interviewed by NBC News, Rodriguez said, "My mom always told me since I was little to always do the right thing, even when nobody's around." This is a perfect example of honesty--doing the right thing when nobody's watching.

- **Learning From Your Mistakes:** Everyone makes mistakes in life, and that's okay. As long as you own up to your mistakes, learn from them and use them as opportunities to grow and teach others what not to do.

- **Self-Discipline:** Self-discipline involves effective time management, staying focused, and avoiding distractions. It means putting your phone away, turning off the TV, or putting your video games away so that you can complete a task. Whether it's homework or working on a project outside school, the more self-discipline you have, the easier it will be to achieve your goals.

- **Achieving Your Goals:** Do you set goals for yourself at the beginning of every year but never achieve them? Accountability is also about setting goals, working out what you must do to achieve them, and then taking action. Sitting around waiting for things to happen will never get you to your destination; what you do will determine your success or failure.

- **Accepting Constructive Criticism:** Constructive criticism is essential to personal development because, if you don't know where you're going wrong, you can't improve. It's not uncommon for people to get offended when criticized because they take it as a personal attack. While it may sting to hear that you're not as good as you thought, it should motivate you to do what needs to be done to become the best version of yourself.

HOW DOES ACCOUNTABILITY IMPACT CONFIDENCE?

When you're accountable, you acknowledge that your decisions determine your life's outcome. Recognizing that you hold the keys to your future boosts your confidence because it gives you a sense of ownership. You no longer feel like a drifter dwelling on external circumstances or blaming others. Instead, you focus on the things you can control and take the necessary steps to overcome challenges and achieve your goals. Accountability impacts confidence in several ways; here are some of them:

You Learn to Embrace the Process

It's not uncommon for people to resent instead of embrace the process while working on their goals. You'll find that the moment you set your heart on achieving something, Murphy's Law shows up at your door. Murphy's Law is a phenomenon where everything that could go wrong will go wrong. But it's also why many people give up; once they encounter obstacles and things start getting difficult, they throw in the towel instead of plowing through. But there is beauty in the process if you learn to change your perspective.

When America's greatest inventor, Thomas Edison, created the incandescent electric light bulb, he failed 10,000 times before perfecting it. During an interview, when asked how he kept going after failing so many times, Edison responded, "I have not failed 10,000 times. I have not failed once. I have succeeded in finding 10,000 ways that will not work. When I have eliminated the ways that will not work, I will find the ways that will work." In other words, there's no such thing as failure; you're simply learning to do something correctly. Embracing the process requires determination and perseverance; you become unstoppable once you develop these qualities.

You Learn to Embrace the Consequences

Your actions have a more significant impact than the present moment; they shape the course of your future. If you decide to scroll on social media instead of studying, the likely consequence is that you'll fail your exams. But when you don't get the grades you'd hoped for, how many will admit to wasting time playing on your phone? Some teenagers don't like accepting responsibility for their actions for several reasons; here are some of them:

- **Fear of Judgement:** Adolescents don't like being judged. You're concerned about what your friends or family members will think of you when you own up to your mistakes. Admitting you made a mistake puts you at risk of being seen in a negative light. And so, instead of owning up to not studying for your exams, you'd rather devise an excuse that takes the heat off you.
- **Pride and Ego:** Accepting responsibility for your actions damages your sense of self when pride and ego are in the way. To avoid this, you play the blame game because it feels better. You'd rather cling to your pride than accept the consequences of your actions.
- **Fear of Punishment:** No one likes getting into trouble, especially teenagers. Whether it's grounding, a loss of

privileges, or some other repercussions, the last thing you want is to deal with the threat of punishment.

You Learn to Forgive Yourself

Forgiveness is defined as making the choice to let go of feelings of resentment, anger, and retribution towards someone you believe has offended you. While forgiving others isn't the easiest thing, it's much harder to forgive ourselves. Everyone makes mistakes, but some people punish themselves unjustly and find it difficult to move on after doing something they're not proud of. We hold ourselves to the highest standards and become hypercritical of our actions. However, accountability teaches us that no one is perfect, and it's okay to make mistakes, but this doesn't mean you're off the hook. If you're willing to learn from your mistakes and accept the consequences, you can move forward and hopefully not repeat the same mistake. When you understand that life is full of lessons and that some of the most powerful lessons you'll learn will come from your mistakes, forgiving yourself becomes much easier.

Accountability Helps You Make Difficult Decisions

When you take ownership of your decisions, you don't blame others or make excuses for your actions; you have control over your life and your choices. Instead of being a passive bystander, you become an active participant in shaping your future. Personal accountability helps you stay true to your values and yourself when considering difficult decisions. Everyone has beliefs and principles that guide them when making choices, even when it's not the most popular or easiest option. It takes a strong person to stick to their beliefs, but it's worth it because it helps build confidence and self-respect.

How to Practice Personal Accountability

Being a teenager can be challenging. Between parental expectations, peer pressure, and school work, sometimes, you feel like you're carrying the weight of the world on your shoulders. However, it's essential to understand that these things prepare you for adulthood. While I encourage you to speak to someone you trust about the things you're struggling with, I also encourage you to change your perspective about these stressors and start seeing them as opportunities for growth. One way you can do this is by practicing personal accountability by doing the following:

Faithful in Little, Faithful in Much

On May 17, 2014, Admiral William H. McRaven delivered a speech to the graduates of The University of Texas at Austin. He stated that while training for the Navy SEALs, they were required to make their beds to perfection every morning. It seemed ridiculous at the time, considering the fact that they were training to go to war. Still, there was hidden wisdom in this mundane exercise. Admiral McRaven stated that when you make your bed in the morning, you will have completed the day's first task. This gives you a sense of pride and encourages you to complete the next task and then the next, until you accomplish everything you need to get done for the day.

As a former Navy SEAL, I thought it was pretty stupid when I first heard this speech. I don't make my bed every morning, and I still manage to accomplish plenty. However, the more I thought about it, the more I realized how the concept applied. Before I joined the Navy, I had trouble getting out of bed in the morning and making it to an 8 a.m. class. I was disorganized and lacked attention to detail. Making my bed in SEAL training, along with room inspections, uniform inspections and other mundane tasks, taught me that little details matter. Through these seemingly unimportant tasks, I learned valuable traits.

In other words, starting your day by making your bed builds momentum and reinforces that the little things in life matter. And how you do the small stuff will determine how you do the big things. His most profound statement during his speech was, "If you want to change the world, start off by making your bed."

Keeping your room in order gives you a sense of pride in yourself and your belongings, and it shows that you have respect for the house you live in. I can guarantee that if you ensure your room is always clean, you will feel better about yourself and more motivated about life.

Help Out Around the House

If you already help out around the house, that's great, but you can always do more. Show your parents you're responsible by taking the initiative to get things done. Your proactiveness will not only show that you want to be more independent; it will also show that you're dependable. Although your parents bought the house for you to live in as a family, you should treat it like it's your house, which means you're responsible for keeping it in order. You might not think there are any benefits to adding more to your schedule and doing mundane tasks like making your bed and keeping your room clean, but there are many.

Here are some of them:

Time Management: In between going to school, extracurricular activities, homework, and hanging out with friends, there's not much time for household chores, which is why you'll need to ensure that you allocate enough time throughout the week to do what you need to do. You'll get the most important things out of the way by managing your time effectively.

Problem Solving: I'm sure you've noticed that homes are challenging to run. There's always something broken that needs to be repaired or a problem that needs to be resolved. By getting more involved with helping out around the house, you'll encounter more problems that you can help resolve.

Communication Skills: The simple act of letting your parents know what you're going to be doing before you do it improves your communication skills. It gives you the confidence required to let others know that you're being proactive, which is a vital skill in the job market.

If you're not used to helping around the house, and you're unsure what to do, ask your parents. But in the meantime, here are some ideas:

- Mow the lawn and keep the front and backyard looking good by weeding and raking leaves.
- Take out the trash and change the garbage bags.
- Clean the windows.
- Clean the floors by vacuuming rugs, carpets and other surfaces.
- Wash dishes and load/unload the dishwasher.
- Load the washing machine, dry the clothes, fold the clothes and put them away.
- Wipe down counters.
- Mop the floors.
- Clean the bathroom, including the toilet, bath/shower, sink, and mirrors.

Get a Summer or a Part-Time Job

Getting a part-time or summer job doesn't just put extra cash in your pocket; it helps you become more responsible and accountable. Taking on paid employment teaches you to manage your time effectively and prioritize your responsibilities. Once you start a job, you'll learn how to juggle different tasks to ensure that you can complete your work duties. It will be important to balance your work hours with school, extracurricular activities and personal commitments.

Having a job requires you to be on time. You'll have shift schedules that you work, and your punctuality will be required. You being late means the person whose shift has ended has to wait for you to arrive, to ensure there is enough staff to do the job.

Taking ownership is an essential part of personal accountability. You're responsible for specific duties and tasks when you have a job. Whether completing projects, serving customers or organizing inventory, you'll learn to take ownership of your work. You'll discover that your actions directly impact the success and performance of the business. This will motivate you to be accountable for your responsibilities and to perform at a high level.

Another skill you will learn when you begin working is financial responsibility. When you start earning money, you become responsible for saving, budgeting and spending wisely. You'll learn about the value of hard work and being responsible for your financial resources.

Wherever you work, you'll face challenges requiring you to think on your feet and find solutions. It might be dealing with a disgruntled customer, a lazy fellow employee or broken equipment. By taking the initiative to resolve issues and find solutions, you demonstrate that you're capable of managing challenges independently and effectively.

Think Before You Act

By thinking before you act, you take a moment to consider the potential consequences of your actions. Some questions to think about before taking action include:

- Does what I'm about to do line up with my values?
- What are the potential consequences of what I'm about to do?
- How will my actions affect the lives of my loved ones?
- Am I considering the feelings of those involved in this decision?

- What alternatives or solutions are there to consider?
- Have I spent enough time thinking this through, or am I acting on impulse?
- What are the long-term implications of my actions?
- How will I feel about this decision tomorrow, next week, or next year?
- What can I learn from similar past experiences?
- What trustworthy and wise person can give me some advice or input about this situation?

Finally, personal accountability is not just a concept; it's a practical tool that can significantly impact your life. As you've read, it will help you develop important life skills that will equip you for academic, personal and professional success. I also want you to remember that what you don't do is just as important as taking action. By choosing not to do what you know you're supposed to do, you rob yourself of becoming the best version of yourself and rob the world of being blessed with your awesomeness. You should start practicing now so that, by the time you're ready for independence, personal accountability will be like second nature.

HERE'S A QUICK RECAP OF EVERYTHING YOU'VE JUST LEARNED:

- Personal accountability is the willingness to take ownership of your decisions, actions, and their consequences. The key components of personal accountability are:

—Taking responsibility
—Being proactive
—Being honest
—Learning from your mistakes
—Practice self-discipline
—Achieving your goals
—Accepting constructive criticism

- Personal accountability impacts confidence because it teaches you how to embrace the process, embrace the consequences of your actions, forgive yourself, and make difficult decisions.
- You can practice personal accountability by keeping your room tidy, helping out around the house, getting a summer or part-time job, and thinking before you act.

Do you struggle to find the right words to express your thoughts, emotions and opinions? Do you admire the people who can stand up in front of crowds and speak with power and authority, but you think that you'd never be able to do the same? If you've answered yes to any of these questions, don't worry; you're not alone. Plenty of teenagers have this issue, and you'll learn how to fix it in the next chapter.

ACTIVITY: BECOME A VOLUNTEER

When you volunteer, you commit to a specific organization or project with a cause bigger than yourself. By following through on these commitments, you develop responsibility as you learn how your involvement directly impacts the success of the project or people you're supporting. Volunteering gives you essential life skills such as time management, problem-solving, leadership, and teamwork skills.

Follow the steps in this activity to find the right volunteer role for you.

- Identify Your Interests and Passions - Narrow down potential volunteer opportunities by thinking about your interests and passions. What issues or causes are you passionate about? Do you enjoy working with animals, children or the elderly? What are the local organizations in your area?
- Research - Begin by researching the local charities, nonprofits, organizations, or community centers that align with your interests. Read through their websites and social media pages

to find information about their missions and volunteer requirements.

- Get Advice From Your School - Schools often have resources dedicated to volunteer opportunities or community service. Your teachers or guidance counselors may be able to help you connect with the organizations you're interested in.
- Attend Volunteer Events - Sometimes, organizations will hold events in your area to recruit volunteers. Attending will give you the opportunity to meet representatives and speak to them about their programs. Search local websites and your school message boards for upcoming events.
- Reach Out to Organizations - Once you've researched and identified organizations of interest, contact them directly. Send an email expressing your enthusiasm to work with them; ask questions about the recruitment process and the commitment you'd need to make to get started.
- Prepare Your Application - If your organization of choice has volunteer positions available, you'll need to complete an application. Be sure to get help from your parents or your guidance counselor at school so that your application is written to the best of your ability. Although you don't get paid for volunteering, organizations still want to ensure they're hiring the person most suitable for the job. Additionally, be prepared to attend an orientation session to learn about the organization's expectations, guidelines, and policies.

Once you've been accepted, you can start volunteering. I encourage you to approach your position with a positive attitude and dedication. Do the job to the best of your ability because not only are you giving back to society and learning essential life skills, but the company will also give you a reference for college if you plan on going.

While you're volunteering, spend time reflecting on your experience. Write about it in your journal. Here are some prompts to get you started.

- What do you enjoy doing the most?
- What skills are you developing?
- What challenges have you faced?
- How does my volunteer work align with my personal beliefs and values?
- What areas can I improve in as a volunteer?
- Is volunteering providing a sense of purpose and fulfillment?
- Is volunteering providing you with a deeper understanding of the needs of others?
- How is your volunteering contributing to the community?
- Are you seeing the impact of your efforts?

CHAPTER 7
FINDING YOUR VOICE

66 *"It's not just what you say; it's also how you say it."* ~
Unknown

COMMUNICATION IS THE CORNERSTONE OF HUMAN CONNECTION AND self-expression. It's one of the most essential skills to master because, without it, you'll sell yourself short in your academic, professional, and personal life. Deep within you, there's a powerful and unique voice, and once you find it, you can change the world. At the moment, you might not feel confident speaking in front of your peers, let alone an audience of complete strangers. However, by the end of this chapter, you'll be equipped with the tools required to turn your hidden voice into a thundering cry that will gain the attention of everyone who hears you.

WHAT IS EFFECTIVE COMMUNICATION?

Effective communication means expressing thoughts and emotions in a way people can understand and don't have to second guess what you're saying. Additionally, the listener is thoroughly engaged in the conversation. The principles of effective communication are a combination of the following:

- Have something important to say when you speak.
- Be curious.
- Be clear.
- Practice active listening.
- Engage with others.
- Consider your body language.

Body Language

When most people think of the word "communication," their first thought is speech. While we do communicate by speaking to others, an essential aspect of communication is body language. According to Albert Mehrabian, a researcher of body language, 55 percent of communication is non-verbal. In other words, we say a lot more with our bodies than we do with our mouths. Our body language is unconscious; we don't think about it, but it speaks loud and clear. For example, you might be the type to plaster a smile on your face and say you're doing great when someone asks, even if you're actually upset about something going on in your life. Despite your smile and what's coming out of your mouth, your body language will tell a different story. You might display rounded shoulders or a furrowed brow, which are signs that you're not doing okay. Having the ability to read body language is like having a superpower because people won't be able to lie to you. But first, you must learn how to be mindful of your own body language.

There's a difference between positive and negative body language. You could be the nicest person in the world, but you come off as standoffish because you have negative body language. To begin, here are some examples of negative and positive body language.

Positive Body Language

Positive body language shows that you're confident, assertive and sure of yourself. Here are some examples of positive body language:

Smiling: A genuine smile radiates positivity and warmth, creating a friendly and inviting atmosphere. A nice smile helps people feel at ease and comfortable.

Making Eye Contact: Making and keeping eye contact demonstrates attentiveness and interest in the conversation. It also shows confidence, sincerity and willingness to connect with others.

Open Posture: Sitting or standing with an open posture, such as uncrossed legs and arms, signals that you're approachable and receptive. You want to listen and are open to communicating with the people in the room.

Mirroring: Mirroring involves subtly copying the body language of the person you're speaking to. It helps you develop a rapport with them. For example, when they pick up their drink, you do the same, or when they tuck their hair behind their ear, you do the same. However, don't overdo it, or it'll become very obvious that you're using the mirroring technique.

Leaning Forward: Slightly leaning into the people you're interacting with shows that you're engaged and interested in what they have to say. It shows that you're focused on the conversation and want to connect on a deeper level.

Open Gestures: Using expressive but natural hand gestures adds clarity, emphasis and enthusiasm to your words, making your message more memorable and engaging.

Confident Posture: Standing tall with your head held high, and your shoulders back shows confidence, self-assurance and competence. A confident posture influences how others perceive you.

Fluid Movements: Express your confidence by moving with ease and fluidity. When the conversation and your movements are flowing, it shows that you're confident in your own skin.

Respect Personal Space: What does respecting personal space have to do with positive body language? It shows that you have social etiquette. While physical contact is a display of affection or friendship, not everyone likes being touched by random people. Encroaching someone's personal space can come across as aggressive and leave them feeling uncomfortable, especially with someone you don't know very well. When you meet someone for the first time, the best thing to do is to give them space. Don't lean in for a hug. Give them enough room so they don't feel as if you're crowding them when they're speaking.

Negative Body Language

Negative body language gives the impression of defensiveness, disinterest, or a closed-off attitude. Negative body language makes it difficult to communicate with others because it creates a barrier between you and the people you're speaking to. Examples of negative body language include:

Invading Personal Space: Standing too close to people you don't know can make them feel uncomfortable. During conversation, you'll be able to gauge how close you can get. It's important to mention that some people will take a few steps back if they feel you're too close. Don't follow their lead and lean in further; stay where you are.

Avoiding Touch: Avoiding touch is different from invading personal space; it involves doing things like avoiding handshakes or hugs. Follow the lead of the person/people you're speaking to. Some people are naturally affectionate and will get offended if you don't reciprocate. So you can shake hands and hug if these displays of physical touch are extended to you.

Fidgeting or Tapping: Fidgeting with your clothes or objects, tapping your fingers or bouncing your legs makes you appear nervous, restless or impatient. It also indicates a lack of focus and can distract the person/people you're speaking to.

Slumped Posture: Hunching over or slouching can communicate a lack of confidence because it's like you're trying to make yourself appear smaller. It can also give the impression that you're unapproachable and uninterested in the conversation.

Scowling or Frowning: Generally, people scowl or frown when angry or frustrated. These facial expressions during a conversation create a negative atmosphere and hinder open communication. It can also show that you don't agree or disapprove of what the person is saying.

Avoiding Eye Contact: Avoiding eye contact makes you appear shy, uncomfortable, or not confident. It can also indicate boredom or a desire to end the conversation.

Crossed Arms/Legs: Crossing your arms or legs creates a barrier between you and the person you're speaking to, making it seem like you don't want to talk. It also gives the impression that you're unapproachable.

Pointed Feet: You can appear as if you literally want to run away from someone if your feet are pointed away from the person you're speaking to. It's an unconscious sign that you don't want to talk and would rather be elsewhere.

THE CONNECTION BETWEEN LISTENING AND COMMUNICATION

Most people listen passively, which means we're only focused on hearing the most important parts of a conversation so that we can remember them later. We are not locked into what the person is saying and might have other thoughts running through our minds, such as what we will eat for dinner or how to respond to what's being said. On the other hand, active listening involves fully engaging in the conversation and paying attention to verbal and nonverbal communication. Active listening is important because it encourages honesty and openness and improves relationships. There are several benefits associated with active listening, including building trust, resolving conflicts and learning to anticipate problems.

Have you ever had a conversation with someone, and it appeared they weren't listening to you? Maybe they were finishing your sentences and getting it wrong, giving you advice you didn't ask for, or interrupting with, "I don't mean to cut you off, but..." to tell you about a similar experience they've had. When you converse with someone like this, you feel unheard and have no desire to confide in them again. The opposite is true when the person is genuinely interested in what you're saying. It's clear they're making a conscious effort to understand things from your perspective.; They validate your feelings and experiences, and this helps create a sense of trust and respect for the person because you feel heard and understood. Additionally, active listening promotes a non-judgmental environment where the speaker feels safe to express themselves without judgment or criticism.

In order to resolve conflicts, you must fully understand what has taken place in a way that is satisfactory to everyone involved. During a disagreement, emotions can be high, perspectives are at odds, and each person has underlying needs to address. In general, conflicts arise from misunderstandings or miscommunication. By giving your full attention to the speaker, you can get to the root of the problem and start working towards a solution. Active listening also involves empathy and shows the other person that their feelings are acknowledged and respected. When people feel understood, they become less defensive and are more likely to compromise.

Active listening enables individuals to gain important information, understand the underlying needs of others, and pick up on subtle cues. Sometimes, people don't always express themselves as they intend. Still, an active listener can tune in and hear what's really being said, even if it's not expressed well. Through active listening, you can identify patterns in communication style and behavior. This will help you identify potential problems based on ongoing issues and past experiences.

YOUR TONE OF VOICE MATTERS

Neutral words can even become offensive if spoken in a demanding, sarcastic or contemptuous tone, causing the listener to feel disrespected and talked down to. When a person's tone of voice is too soft, they're looked at as lacking confidence. But a person with a boisterous, loud voice is seen as aggressive. Your tone is essential if you want to get your message across correctly. Your tone of voice helps influence others, make connections and build rapport. Here are some examples of tones of voice:

Formal: A formal tone involves precise vocabulary, proper grammar, and a respectful and professional demeanor. You would use a formal tone of voice if you were speaking to someone like a school principal or interviewing for a job.

Informal: An informal tone of voice is used when speaking to friends, family members, or just having a general conversation with someone you know. It can include using abbreviations like 'ASAP' or a casual greeting such as 'Hey.' This language is less structured and implies that there's familiarity between you and the person you're speaking to.

Assertive: An assertive tone is when the language is confident and firm and expresses a sense of expectation and urgency. This clear and straightforward communication leaves no room for misunderstanding or ambiguity. The speaker clearly states their expectations and requests that the listener take action within a specific time frame.

Factual: A factual tone requires objectivity and avoiding subjective interpretations or personal biases. It includes sticking to the facts without adding emotions or personal opinions.

Questioning: A questioning tone of voice is when your language conveys a sense of uncertainty, inquiry, or curiosity; you're engaging in conversation because you want clarity about something.

HOW EFFECTIVE COMMUNICATION BOOSTS CONFIDENCE

When we speak to people, most of us are not thinking about how our confidence plays a role in the conversation. However, It's very easy to detect a lack of confidence, insecurity, and discomfort by the way a person speaks, even if you're not conscious of it. When people speak, you pay attention to the words coming out of their mouth, their tone, and their body language. When there's a mismatch, you get a "gut feeling" that something isn't right. At that point, you either feel that the person isn't telling the whole truth or that they're lying. But most of the time, the problem is that they lack confidence.

When you speak with confidence, you find it easier to express yourself. Your thoughts are clear, and the words form in a way that forces the listener to hear you even if they don't want to. Duncan's story is a great example of how effective communication can boost your confidence.

Duncan's Story – An 18-Year-Old Boy From Ojai, California

"During high school, I was probably the quietest kid in my class. Even after my voice broke, I had a high-pitched voice that didn't sound very masculine. Needless to say, I was bullied relentlessly for it because the kids said I sounded like a girl. Unfortunately for me, one of my assignments involved giving a formal reading. Not only did I have to stand up in front of the bullies and speak, but it was recorded! Well, guess what happened? I froze. I completely lost my voice, and

I couldn't say anything at all. I got a D for that assignment, which gave the other kids additional ammunition to tease me.

I went home that evening in tears. My parents comforted me as much as they could, but they couldn't change my voice. That night, my dad gave me some advice that stirred me into action. He said, "Son, I know you don't sound like other boys, but that's what makes you special. Your voice is different; you'd rather read a book than kick and that's okay. Own who you are, Duncan. Your mother and I are proud of you because you're a wonderful young man. But you can't allow other people to steal your joy just because they have a problem with who you are. I'm not telling you to fight back with your fists, but my father told me that success is the greatest revenge you'll ever have."

So, we devised a plan and decided that I would use my voice to become the captain of the debate team. I loved reading and had insight into things that most people knew nothing about. So that's exactly what I did. I joined the debate team. Not only did I join the debate team, but I also began reading about and studying the greatest speakers in the world and learning about effective communication. I spent my evenings preparing for my debates and practicing my speaking skills. And guess what? Within 18 months, I was the captain of the debate team! To add insult to injury for the kids that made fun of me, I was valedictorian of my class and gave the farewell speech at graduation. I got a standing ovation and a thunderous applause!

Today, I'm happy, healthy and proud of my unique voice. Everyone I come into contact with loves it because I love it. I learned to love who I am, and improving my communication skills was the beginning of my confidence journey. So my message to you is don't let anyone convince you you're not good enough. And even if you don't plan on becoming a speaker, developing your communication skills will serve you well. I can vouch for that"!

TIPS ON HOW TO COMMUNICATE WITH CONFIDENCE

Learning how to communicate with confidence takes time. Duncan didn't become the captain of the school's debate team overnight. He spent 18 months practicing! If you want to improve your communication skills, it will take dedication.

Whether we pay attention to it or not, everyone has an inner voice. It's like a record player lingering in the background. Unfortunately, that voice isn't a kind, caring voice of reason for most of us. It's more like the evil twin telling us we're not good enough. The good news is that you can control that voice through practice. You will begin to control it if you speak to yourself with kindness and encouragement. But if you talk to yourself with disdain, it will manifest as low self-esteem. The good news is you can control your inner voice by using the tips below.

Spend Time Alone: Tune into your inner thoughts. Turn off your devices, eliminate distractions, and focus on your thoughts. This is a great time to journal, which will help you get to know yourself better.

Focus on the Present: Most people spend their time either regretting the past or worrying about the future. Neither of these is productive because you can't change the past or determine what will happen in the future. Focusing on the present moment can improve mental clarity, reduce stress, and improve emotional well-being. When you regret past mistakes or worry about the future, bring yourself back to the present moment by focusing on what you're doing at that time.

Learn to be Your Own Cheerleader: Life is hard and at times can be lonely. Even if we have others around us who care about us, they may not know what we are facing. Sometimes, we need to be that friend to ourselves and encourage ourselves. We have to cheer ourselves on and draw from past wins to keep pushing forward. If we can't remember a past win, then we just need to make it through the challenge directly in front of us.

Change Your Words to Change Your Thinking: Affirmations are a great way to turn off your negative inner voice and start speaking to yourself with positivity. Start your day by looking in the mirror and saying something positive about yourself. Some examples of positive affirmations include:

- "I am capable of being successful, because I am capable of putting in the required effort and work."
- "I cannot control others, but I can control myself."
- "I can do my best today."
- "Failing doesn't make me a failure; it is a powerful way to learn."
- "I am capable of achieving my goals and fulfilling my dreams."

Practice Active Listening: As I mentioned earlier, active listening is an important communication skill because it encourages honesty and openness and improves relationships. Next time you're in a conversation with a friend, give them your full attention. Put your phone and other devices away. If other stuff is happening in the room, ignore it and give your full attention to the person speaking.

Try to keep your thoughts to yourself until the speaker has expressed themselves fully. If they stop speaking and you're unsure whether they've said everything they need to say, ask a question to gain clarity on what you just heard. Additionally, only give advice about the situation if the person asks.

Approach the conversation with an open mind and eliminate any preconceived notions you might have about the subject. For example, if your friend wants to speak to you about how pollution is destroying the planet, but it's not something you care about and you think that environmentalists are slightly unhinged, leave your opinions at the door and let your friend talk. You might discover something you didn't know, which could change your mind about the topic. Also, making assumptions insults the person speaking because, by jumping to conclusions, you're dismissing the person's life experiences. It might not mean anything to you, but it means something to them.

Nonverbal cues such as nodding your head, making facial expressions, and smiling show that you're listening and fully engaged in the conversation. Once the person has finished speaking, show that you've understood what was said by repeating what was said in your own words. If you've misunderstood anything, the speaker will let you know.

So next time you're having a conversation with someone, think about the situation from their perspective and not yours. Do your best to walk in their shoes, tap into their emotions, and feel what they're feeling. The more a person feels understood, the more they'll open up to you, which will strengthen your relationship.

Add Humor: Everyone is funny in their own way, and you can't be serious all the time. You may not be comedian-level funny, but there are quirks about you that your friends and family members find endearing. Tap into those quirks and use them when you're speaking to people. Also, don't shy away from turning the joke on yourself; it shows that you don't take yourself too seriously and can help break the ice and ease the tension in the air.

Know Your Subject: Some people are not confident presenting, because they didn't prepare properly. If you're asked to give a presentation at school, the best way to appear more confident (even if you're nervous) is to know what you're talking about. Spend a lot of time researching the information and verifying the facts. Once you've gathered all the research, practice until you're familiar with the content. When you're fully prepared, you'll always make a good impression, even if you're not the most confident person.

Effective communication is a powerful tool that improves your interactions with friends and loved ones and boosts your confidence. As you continue on your journey of self-discovery and personal growth, remember that effective communication is more than the words you choose to speak; it is about the respect, empathy, kindness and compassion we bring to our interactions.

HERE'S A QUICK RECAP OF WHAT YOU'VE LEARNED IN THIS CHAPTER:

- The principles of effective communication are to have something important to say when you speak, be curious, be clear, practice active listening, engage with others, and consider your body language.
- Positive body language shows you're confident, assertive and sure of yourself.
- Negative body language gives the impression of defensiveness, disinterest or a closed-off attitude.
- Active listening builds trust, resolves conflicts and helps you anticipate problems.
- Your tone of voice matters when speaking; therefore, make sure your voice matches the message you want to deliver.
- You can practice communicating with confidence by developing your inner voice, practicing active listening, adding humor and knowing your subject.

If you've been implementing the strategies you're reading about, by this point, you should be feeling at least a little bit more confident. If not, don't worry, keep practicing, don't rush the process, you'll get there when you get there. The final chapter is about living an authentic life which is perhaps one of the most difficult things to do when we live in a world that values conformity. An authentic life is a liberated life, free from the judgements of others, but it takes confidence to achieve it. In the final chapter, I'll show you how.

ACTIVITY: THE COMMUNICATION CIRCLE

Most teenagers have the same struggles, and communication is one of them. Getting together with a group of people your age to practice your communication skills is a great way to develop confidence in this area.

Instructions:

Step 1: Select a few friends you trust and ask them to spend a couple of days reading Chapter 7.

Step 2: Arrange to meet at someone's house for a hangout. Everyone brings a snack to share and a question to put into the discussion jar (any bowl or jar will do!)

Step 3: Start by explaining the guidelines for the activity. A topic is selected, and you all take turns speaking while the others listen respectfully. After each person has finished speaking, you can have a group discussion about what was said. Encourage open and honest conversation, and stress the importance of empathy and kindness.

Step 4: Finish with a group discussion about how the activity went, and give everyone the chance to share their experience and the lessons learned.

Before everyone leaves, decide on a regular meeting time for future meet-ups, to work on building your conversation skills. It can be monthly or even weekly if you find it helpful, but you should at least try to meet a few times for the activity to really be effective.

CHAPTER 8
LIVING A LIFE OF PURPOSE

 "Watch over your heart with all diligence, For from it flow the springs of life."

-Proverbs 4:23

I TOTALLY GET IT. IT'S HARD BEING A TEENAGER. THERE ARE SO MANY external influences that sometimes, you don't know where you belong. You are unique, and whatever gifts and talents you were born with were given to you so that you could be a blessing to others.

It's common to feel the need to fit into society's norms and standards or to live up to other people's expectations of us. But if we want to become confident and live authentically, we sometimes must walk a different path.

START WITH THE END IN MIND

At the end of your life, how will you answer these three questions? Who did I love, who loved me and did I live a life of meaning? If we frame our actions through these three questions, we will be more intentional in the now, the present. Doing this allows us to take a long-term perspective on short-term goals.

You're on a mission to find out what truly matters, what you're passionate about, and what sets your heart on fire. Authenticity is about embracing what makes you unique. It's about embracing your interests, passions, and quirks, even if they don't align with what's considered normal. It's like showing up to school wearing a neon-colored hoodie when everyone else is wearing a gray one. Guess who they'll be staring at? They'll be staring at you, because you clearly stand out and don't look like all the others.

When you stay true to ethical values, you're guided by a moral compass and don't allow the status quo to sway you. Many people think that having morals and values is just doing what feels right to them at the time. The problem with this is that feelings often change. Treating our feelings as if they are moral truths and using them to live our lives is similar to trying to navigate in the wilderness with a broken compass. We can get lucky sometimes, but more often than not, we will be lost.

Living a life of purpose isn't easy. It means being vulnerable, showing the world your true self, exposing your soul, and saying, "Hey world, this is me!"

But you know what? It's totally worth it, because you cut out every-thing that doesn't really matter, and you only attract the people who like you for you instead of the person they think you are or want you to be. Think about that for a minute; imagine being friends with someone for years only to discover that they were faking who they were all along. If you'd known who they really were, you wouldn't have made friends with them in the first place. Well, that's what happens when you don't live an authentic life; you attract all the wrong people.

FIND YOUR CALLING AND CHANGE THE WORLD

We all have unique gifts and talents we can use to make the world a better place. The challenging part is figuring out what they are and how to use them. We sometimes discover our gifts through other people or when we push ourselves outside our comfort zones. What are you naturally good at? What do you learn quickly? What is fun for you to learn? Where do you have aptitude?

It's easy to focus on our weaknesses, and sometimes we need to do this. But if we just focus on the things we lack, we can overlook our gifts and talents and never find them.

If you haven't found your gifts and talents yet, that's okay; you're not alone. It took me a while to figure out what mine were and how to use them, and I am still working on improving them. Here is how you can start to find yours.

Get Started on Something

If you sit around and wait, it's unlikely that you will ever figure out your gifts and talents. So, get started on something. It could be anything. What's something that interests you? What's something you've always wanted to do but were afraid you might fail? What is something others have told you that you would be good at? You can always shift focus to something else along the way, but get started with something.

Was This My Best Work?

We live in a time when mediocrity is accepted and even expected. If you want to find your gifts and make a difference, you must break free from mediocrity. In school, those who do well are often labeled as "overachievers,', "nerds,' "teacher's pets," etc. The truth is that these people are jealous or just plain lazy, and people who work hard and do their best make the lazy people look, well, lazy. They would rather drag you down to their level than allow you to rise above and outperform them. It's not easy, but you must ignore these labels and ask yourself one simple question. Was this the best I could do? If the answer is yes, then you've done all you can. If the answer is no, do it over so that your answer is yes. Each time you do something, do your best and improve each time you do it again. When we push ourselves this way, we will quickly find the areas where we excel.

Find a Mentor

This idea of finding answers within ourselves has baffled me. Imagine having all the parts to an engine in front of you, and you have two options. Option one is to find the answers within yourself to assemble it. Option two is you have an experienced mechanic and an instruction manual to help you assemble it. I don't know about you, but I am picking option two every time. Life is much more complicated than an engine, and we should learn from those with more experience than us. We can learn something from everyone. Sometimes we learn what to do, and sometimes we learn what not to do. We can also learn through reading, watching videos, etc., but we must always consider the source of our information.

Have you ever heard of an apprentice? Not long ago, trades were dominated by master craftsmen, merchants, etc. Each of these masters would have one or more apprentices. The apprentice would work under the master and learn the trade. After many years, the apprentice would become the master. Oftentimes, the apprentices would be the children of the craftsman or merchant. Children often had little choice about what their profession would be. For the most part, whatever their parent's trade was would also be theirs.

I'm not saying we should go back to this model, but there are some valuable insights that can be gained from this historical model.

1. There are people who are masters of the thing we want to be good at.

107

2. We should find these people and learn from them.
3. Only after we've learned from them can we become masters in the field.
4. Once we've mastered a field, we can bring our own creativity to it and impact the world.

THREE MONSTERS THAT STAND IN OUR WAY

On our path to becoming confident, finding our gifts and achieving our goals, three monsters are standing in our way: distraction, resistance and victimhood. Let's take a look at them and learn how to recognize and conquer them. I have learned that awareness is the first step.

Distraction

Have you ever tried to complete a school assignment, but after an hour, you realize that you haven't made any progress? This is often a result of distraction. We live in a world full of distractions, and if we're going to reach our potential, we must learn to focus. I challenge you to start by recognizing when you are distracted. As you get better at recognizing distractions, you'll improve your focus.

Resistance

This is that little voice saying, "I can't do it." You are not the only one this happens to. It happens to all of us at some level. If we listen to this voice, we don't try our best or even try at all. Counter that resistance by taking the first step and trying your best. Let's say you struggle with a subject in school and your first thought is, "I won't get a good grade anyway." Counter this thought by working your hardest to learn the subject. While this won't guarantee a good grade in the short term, if you do it consistently, you'll notice significant improvement in the long term.

Victimhood

Victimhood says things like life isn't fair, my teacher doesn't like me, I deserve it, etc. It's not that these things aren't sometimes true. It's that these things are outside of our control. We cannot control the world around us. We can only control our response. If we play the victim, then we only limit ourselves. When we take responsibility for ourselves and work on improving every day, we can move past this victim mentality and get in the driver's seat towards our goals. Life isn't fair, and everyone isn't going to like us. The sooner we realize that, the faster we will grow in confidence.

PUTTING IT ALL TOGETHER

Now that you've read through eight chapters full of strategies to help you become more confident, the final step is to put everything together in the context of living your best life with authenticity. Here's how:

Unleashing the Power Within

Authenticity and confidence go hand in hand. You can't achieve one without the other. As you've just read, living as your authentic self involves breaking free from conformity and showing up as your true self. Who you are isn't going to resonate with everyone, and that's okay. Remember, it's not about living to please people but rather living to become the best version of yourself and an asset to the world. It takes confidence to decide that you're not going to be like everyone else and that you're going to be unique and different without giving in to peer pressure. Not all teenagers can do this. Heck, not all adults can even do this, so pat yourself on the back for making this decision. Confidence is about accepting yourself for who you are, including your flaws and imperfections. Still, the reality is that it's easier said than done, and one of the reasons for this is that you may have become accustomed to patterns of negative thinking.

Overcoming Negative Thinking

Everything starts in the mind. You picked up this book because you decided that you wanted to become more confident. You decided to improve your life, and I applaud you for that. Unfortunately, your mind can also work against you; there are many reasons why teenagers suffer from low self-esteem, and one reason is because of negative thinking. Because they're constantly telling themselves that they're not good enough, they believe it, and everything they do reflects their mindset.

This typically includes self-sabotaging behaviors such as a victim mentality, seeking constant validation, procrastination, and turning to destructive habits such as smoking and drinking. Living an authentic life requires you to think positively so that you're not focused on your shortcomings or what others think about you. This is your time. This is your moment. However, you'll need to free yourself from the shackles that have been placed on your mind.

Discovering Your Strengths

Everyone has strengths, and that includes you. It may not feel like it right now because you're not in the right frame of mind, but you are equipped with your own set of strengths. You might be in a difficult phase of your life, where everything seems like a never-ending uphill struggle, but finding and embracing your gifts and talents is like a superpower that will catapult you to the next level. An essential part of authenticity is using your strengths. Using your natural abilities is a celebration of your uniqueness and individuality. It's like shining a spotlight on what makes you unique and owning it. When you're doing what you do best, your confidence soars because you begin to trust your abilities and believe in yourself, which spills over into all areas of your life. When you utilize your strengths, you tap into a wellspring of passions and motivations that bring purpose and meaning to your life, which drives you to pursue your dreams.

Breaking Free From Limiting Beliefs

Limiting beliefs are like invisible barriers that hold you back from embracing your authentic self. They're those sneaky thoughts that whisper, "You'll never succeed," or "You're not good enough." But guess what? You can silence those doubts and rewrite your narrative. By breaking free from limiting beliefs, you let go of the fear of judgment and embrace everything about yourself – the good and the bad. By challenging and discarding these beliefs, you begin to recognize your self-worth, and your newfound confidence will empower you to live an authentic life. Limiting beliefs can steer you away from your passions and dreams, causing you to settle for a life that doesn't align with your values. Think about what you really desire and decide that you're going to go after those things with everything you've got.

Embrace Your Uniqueness

Embracing one's uniqueness as a teenager is a transformative journey. Often, teenagers find themselves grappling with insecurities as they navigate a world that seems to prioritize conformity. The very aspects that set them apart from the crowd, their quirks, passions, and individuality, are frequently suppressed in fear of not fitting into popular culture. However, it's essential to understand that these differences are not weaknesses but strengths waiting to be celebrated.

When teenagers choose to embrace their uniqueness, they embark on a path towards authenticity. They discover that their distinctive qualities are what make them extraordinary and memorable. These unique traits are the building blocks of self-confidence and self-acceptance, paving the way for more meaningful relationships and a deeper understanding of themselves.

Furthermore, embracing one's uniqueness enables teenagers to contribute to the world in a way that only they can. It fosters creativity, innovation, and a sense of purpose. By being true to themselves, teenagers inspire others to do the same, creating a ripple effect of authenticity and empowerment in their communities.

While it may be challenging to break away from the mold, those who dare to embrace their uniqueness embark on a fulfilling journey towards living an authentic life, unlocking their true potential, and making a positive impact on the world around them.

Own Your Story

Taking personal responsibility is like holding the steering wheel of your own life, guiding you toward a future that truly aligns with your values and aspirations, all while staying true to your unique self. Living authentically means being real, honest and unapologetically you. This journey begins with personal accountability, where you make a pact with yourself to honor your commitments.

When you own your story, you're in control of your narrative. It's about more than just keeping promises; it's about forging trust, integrity, and self-respect. By being accountable, you build a solid foundation for your authentic life journey.

To truly embrace this, start with introspection. Reflect on your thoughts, actions, and behaviors with genuine self-awareness. Be open about the areas where you want to grow and the patterns that might be holding you back. Then, take deliberate steps to break free from those barriers. By owning your story and taking responsibility, you're embarking on a meaningful path to living your most authentic, unique, and fulfilling life as a teenager today.

Find Your Voice

Communicating effectively helps you express your thoughts, feelings and ideas. Finding your voice and sharing your thoughts with others allows them to see and understand you for who you truly are. Do you want to have better relationships with your friends and family members? Communication is the glue that keeps you connected with your loved ones. You build genuine connections on trust, understanding and empathy by expressing yourself authentically and listening actively. By connecting with people on a deeper level, you form authentic bonds that will enrich your life and help you become a confident and well-rounded person.

Now that you've put all the puzzle pieces together, it's time to start taking action towards living an authentic life. You've learned that being authentic takes courage. It means stepping out of your comfort zone, facing your fears, and embracing your vulnerabilities. Remember, you can shape your life and create a future that aligns with your values. Follow your dreams, embrace your passions, and don't be afraid to let your true colors shine. Be unapologetically you. Be bold and courageous, because the world needs your authentic self!

ACTIVITY: DISCOVER YOUR CALLING AND MAKE A DIFFERENCE

Objective: This self-guided activity is designed to help you reflect on your passions, purpose, and how you can contribute positively to the world.

Materials Needed:

1. A journal or notebook.

2. Pen or pencil.

Instructions:

Self-Reflection and Passion Discovery

Step 1: Set the Mood

Find a quiet and comfortable place where you won't be disturbed. Put away all distractions (cell phones!) and take a few deep breaths to center yourself and clear your mind.

Step 2: Create a Mind Map

Begin by creating a mind map in your journal. In the center, write your name. Then, branch out with words or phrases that represent your interests, hobbies, skills, and values. Think about what truly excites and motivates you. Spend about 20-30 minutes on this.

Step 3: Personal Values Assessment

List out common values or create your own list. Rank these values from most to least important to you. Take your time with this and reflect on why certain values matter to you.

Step 4: Craft a Mission Statement

Write a personal mission statement. Describe your ideal future and focus on how you want to make a difference in the world. It can be a few sentences or a short paragraph.

Step 5: Identify your passions

Brainstorm various topics that resonate with your values and vision and spark emotion within you. Try to come up with 5-10 topics. Choose one or more issues that you're passionate about to dive deeper into.

Step 6: Research and Knowledge Gathering

Take some time to research your chosen social issue(s). Use books, articles, websites, or any other resources available to gather information. Spend at least 30-45 minutes on this.

Step 7: Create an Action Plan

In your journal, outline a simple plan of action. Describe the specific steps you can take to make a positive impact on the topics you are passionate about. This plan should include short-term and long-term goals.

Step 8: Review and Commit

Review your mind map, personal values, mission statement, and an action plan to get involved. Reflect on the connections between your passions, purpose, and your potential to make a difference. Make a commitment to yourself to start working on your action plan.

This self-guided activity aims to help you discover your passions, clarify your purpose, and inspire you to take meaningful steps toward making a positive impact on the world. Remember that change starts with you, and your actions, no matter how small, can contribute to a better world.

CONCLUSION

CONGRATULATIONS! YOU MADE IT TO THE END OF THE BOOK. YOUR determination to finish reading this book indicates that you're serious about changing your mindset and becoming confident and self-assured. And for that, we're incredibly proud of you, because that's what we want for you, too.

We live in the greatest era in history. Everything we could ever want to buy or to learn is available at the click of a button. But there are some things you can't buy, and confidence is one of them. It's a super-power that must be earned, and the only way to earn it is to work for it. The strategies you've read about in this book are powerful beyond measure, but to reap their full benefits, you must put them to use. You've got to practice being confident, and even when you become confident, you've got to keep practicing.

Let me be real with you for a moment. During this journey, there will be times when the voice of doubt will whisper in your ear, urging you to give up, and frustration will threaten to consume you. But I want to remind you that true growth lies beyond those barriers of fear and uncertainty. Embrace the wisdom of perseverance—the eternal flame that will keep you going even when the road seems impossibly steep. Remember that failures and setbacks are not an indication of your worth, but rather, they're opportunities for learning and growth. Obstacles are like leveling up in a video game. The more challenges you face, the stronger and more confident you become.

Be patient with yourself as you master the art of confidence, trust the process, and believe in the power of your potential. Even though you might not feel like it now, you have what it takes. Think about building confidence like you're going to the gym. You're not going to see results immediately, but below the surface, your body is changing. Your muscles are slowly growing, the fat is melting, and your skin is tightening. Keep doing those reps and eating the right foods, and within a few months, you'll see the benefits of your hard work. Consistency is key; don't rush through the strategies you've read about. Take small daily steps and intentional actions, and you will experience a gradual evolution. If you persevere, you'll be a completely different person a year from now--a better person. Your abilities can be improved through hard work and dedication. Develop a thirst for knowledge; use it like a passport to different worlds. By seeking knowledge, you break free from the constraints of your immediate environment and gain a broader perspective on life. You discover new ways of thinking and ideas that challenge your current mindset. Your potential is limitless, and there are no boundaries to what you can achieve. Become more open to taking on challenges, exploring new opportunities, and stepping into the unknown. Your confidence will blossom as you dare to dream big and believe in your ability to make those dreams a reality.

As a teenager, it's easy to get caught up in the comparison game—believing you're the only one who doesn't have it all together and hasn't figured out life yet. The reality is that most people your age are stumbling in the shadows of self-doubt; everyone is a work in progress. Confidence is not an endpoint. It's a lifelong journey of growth and self-discovery.

In closing, I want to leave you with a resounding message of empowerment and self-discovery. As you journey through life, remember to carefully choose the company you keep. True friends are those who lift you higher, supporting your dreams and aspirations. They celebrate your uniqueness rather than stifling it. In a world that often pressures you to conform, always remember that the true essence of coolness lies in standing out and embracing your authentic self.

Confidence isn't rooted in perfection. It's the art of embracing your imperfections while continually striving to become a better version of yourself. The wisdom you've gathered on this journey is a precious treasure, a guiding light that will lead you toward your own greatness.

The title of this book, "Teen Confidence Unlocked," symbolizes the key you now hold to unlock your potential and inner strength. The world eagerly awaits your presence, and you possess the extraordinary power to illuminate every corner of it with your vibrant, authentic self. Embrace this adventure with an open heart and the knowledge that you are uniquely equipped to create a positive impact. As you step into your light, you not only unlock your own potential but also inspire others to do the same. So go forth, confident and unapologetically you, and let your light shine as a beacon for others to follow. Your journey has just begun, and the world is better for it.

UNLOCK THE POTENTIAL OF TOMORROW'S LEADERS!

 "Confidence is silent, insecurities are loud." - Anonymous

EMPOWERING TEENS WITH CONFIDENCE IS A GIFT THAT KEEPS ON GIVING. As you delve into the pages of "Teen Confidence Unlocked," we hope you're inspired and enlightened by what you find. And now, we have a small favor to ask: **Would you be willing to inspire a teen you've never met, without spending a dime or seeking any recognition?**

If you're nodding in agreement, we have a heartfelt request on behalf of a young teen you might have never met and even the teens that you do know.

They might be just like you were during your teenage years: full of dreams, seeking affirmation, and looking for a light to guide them into their next phase of life. This is where your words can make a difference.

To further our mission of boosting the confidence of young adults, **we need your voice**. This is where you come in. Most people do, in fact, judge a book by their covers (and its reviews!), we humbly request that you spare a minute to post an honest review. It's a small gesture that can have a profound impact.

Your review has the potential to:

- Encourage a teen to believe in themselves.
- Help young students find their true potential.
- Allow someone to embark on a journey of self-discovery.
- Transform countless lives in ways you can't even imagine.
- Light up someone's world with a new vision for their future.

All it takes is a minute of your time to leave a review.

If you are on Audible - hit the three dots at the top right of your device, click rate & review, then leave a few sentences about the book with a star rating.

If you are on Kindle or an e-reader - scroll to the bottom of the book then swipe up and it will prompt you to leave a review.

If for some reason these tactics have changes, simply go to Amazon (or wherever you purchased the book) and leave a review right on the books page.

WITH IMMENSE GRATITUDE,

Chad and Kristi Metcalf

JOIN OUR COMMUNITY

MENTAL TOUGHNESS
AND CONFIDENCE

👍 **SCAN ME** ⨍

If you enjoyed this book, you are the perfect fit to join our community of teens, athletes, parents and coaches passionate about *Building Mental Toughness and Confidence.*

Click here to join the Facebook Group! or use the QR code.

After you join, feel free to introduce yourself. I look forward to hearing about your progress and journey as you start building your mindset. See you in the Facebook Group!

SOCIAL MEDIA LINKS

MENTAL TOUGHNESS
AND CONFIDENCE

Instagram: @chad__metcalf

TikTok: @chad__metcalf

YouTube @chadmetcalf

Spotify - Chad Metcalf

REFERENCES

+TALK, G. (2015, MARCH 23). *MIRROR EXERCISE — DR CAROL*. DR Carol. https://dr-carol.com/category/mirror-exercise/

4 Strategies to Help Teens Learn Accountability | Banner. (n.d.-a). https://www.bannerhealth.com/healthcareblog/advise-me/use-these-4-proven-strategies-to-help-teens-learn-accountability

9 Traits Self-Confident People Have in Common | The American Society of Administrative Professionals. (2023). *ASAP*. https://www.asaporg.com/efficiency-skills/9-traits-self-confident-people-have-in-common

10 common Negative thinking Patterns and 5 Steps for change. (n.d.). https://www.familycentre.org/news/post/10-common-negative-thinking-patterns-and-5-steps-for-change

10 things Genuinely confident people do differently. (2021a, August 13). Main. https://www.td.org/insights/10-things-genuinely-confident-people-do-differently

10 ways to practice self-acceptance. (2023a, January 13). Kids Help Phone. https://kidshelpphone.ca/get-info/10-ways-practice-self-acceptance/

24 Volunteer ideas for Teens. (2021, March 16). YMCA. https://www.ymca.org/blog/articles/24-volunteer-ideas-for-teens

A moment for Me: Self-Compassion break for teens and students. (2023, August 28). Greater Good in Education. https://ggie.berkeley.edu/practice/a-moment-for-me-a-self-compassion-break-for-teens/

A parent's story about self-confidence - ReachOut Parents. (n.d.). https://parents.au.reachout.com/skills-to-build/wellbeing/a-parents-story-about-self-confidence

A quote by Eckhart Tolle. (n.d.). https://www.goodreads.com/quotes/302398-only-the-truth-of-who-you-are-if-realized-will

A quote by Mary Kay Ash. (n.d.). https://www.goodreads.com/quotes/405451-don-t-limit-yourself-many-people-limit-themselves-to-what-they

A quote by Molière. (n.d.). https://www.goodreads.com/quotes/49256-it-is-not-only-what-we-do-but-also-what

Aaron. (2023, March 14). How to Identify Negative Core Beliefs and challenge them. *The British Association of Anger Management.* https://www.angermanage.co.uk/how-to-identify-negative-core-beliefs-and-challenge-them-once-and-for-all/

Ackerman, C. E., MA. (2023a). What is Self-Acceptance? 25 Exercises + definition & quotes. *PositivePsychology.com.* https://positivepsychology.com/self-acceptance/

Ackerman, C. E., MA. (2023c). What is Self-Image in Psychology? How Do We Improve it? *PositivePsychology.com.* https://positivepsychology.com/self-image/

Active listening with pre-teens and teenagers. (2021, September 7). Raising Children Network. https://raisingchildren.net.au/pre-teens/communicating-relationships/communicating/active-listening

Admin. (2019a, November 14). *Why Finding Your Authentic Self Is So Important For Teens | Cathy Lander-Goldberg | Episode 98 - Mighty Parenting.* Mighty Parenting. https://mightyparenting.com/why-finding-your-authentic-self-is-so-important-for-teens-cathy-lander-goldberg-episode-98/

Admin. (2022, September 22). *Importance of identifying your strengths and weaknesses - make me better.* Make Me Better. https://www.make-mebetter.net/importance-of-identifying-your-strengths-and-weaknesses/

Advekit. (n.d.). Advekit. https://www.advekit.com/blogs/what-causes-low-self-esteem

AgeEnvy. (2020a, May 11). *May is National Teen Self-Esteem Month | Lifeworks Counseling Center.* Lifeworks. https://lifeworkscc.com/may-national-teen-self-esteem-month

Alhashmi, A. K. (n.d.-a). 25 powerful coaching questions to discover your strengths & talents. *www.linkedin.com.* https://www.linkedin.com/pulse/25-powerful-coaching-questions-discover-your-strengths-ali-khaled

Allen, L. (2019, July 3). Embracing individuality: Why there's power in being fully you. *ADOA.* https://www.adoaa.org/post/embrac-ing-individuality-why-there-s-power-in-being-fully-you#:~:text=When%20one%20person%20em-braces%20and,has%20different%20perspectives%20and%20pref-erences.

An Authentic Life – 25 Ways to Live it. (n.d.). https://mindbodyspirit-coaching.com/personal-leadership/an-authentic-life-25-ways-to-live-it

Asana, T. (2023, January 3). 10 Limiting Beliefs And How to Overcome Them [2023] • Asana. *Asana.* https://asana.com/resources/limiting-beliefs

Aswell, S. (2020, August 20). *I use this 5-Minute therapy technique every day for my anxiety.* Healthline. https://www.healthline.com/health/mental-health/self-talk-exercises#How-to-use-the-5-minute-triple-column-technique-

Authenticity (Stanford Encyclopedia of Philosophy). (2020, February 20). https://plato.stanford.edu/entries/authenticity/

Author. (n.d.). *Surround yourself with good people.* Life, Hope & Truth. https://lifehopeandtruth.com/life/blog/surround-yourself-with-good-people/

Automatic Thoughts: How to identify and fix them. (n.d.). https://www.betterup.com/blog/automatic-thoughts

Basic teen Self-Compassion — teen Self-Compassion. (n.d.). Teen Self-Compassion. https://teenselfcompassion.org/basic-teen-selfcompassion

Being Your Authentic Self Is Easier Said than Done but Worth It. (n.d.). https://www.betterup.com/blog/authentic-self

biglifejournal.com. (n.d.). *How to Help Teens Set Effective Goals (Tips & Templates).* Big Life Journal. https://biglifejournal.com/blogs/blog/guide-effective-goal-setting-teens-template-worksheet

Bl. (n.d.). *Reddit - Dive into anything.* https://www.reddit.com/r/AskMen/comments/q9zpht/from_where_does_generally_very_low_self_esteem_in/

Bradberry, T. (2015, April 2). 12 things Truly confident people do differently. *Forbes.* https://www.forbes.com/sites/travisbradberry/2015/04/01/12-things-truly-confident-people-do-differently/?sh=161a114a4766

British Heart Foundation. (2023, December 6). Active listening. *https://www.bhf.org.uk/informationsupport/heart-matters-magazine/wellbeing/how-to-talk-about-health-problems/active-listening.* https://www.bhf.org.uk/informationsupport/heart-matters-magazine/wellbeing/how-to-talk-about-health-problems/active-listening

Bryant, C. D. (n.d.). *Quote for teens on communication skills | Truth be told quotes.* Truth Be Told Quotes. https://truthbetoldquotes.com/quotes-teens/quote-what-you-say-how-say-it.html

Burk, A. (2023, January 2). *A Beginner's Guide to Goal Setting for Teens - Powerful Youth.* Powerful Youth. https://powerfulyouth.com/beginners-guide-goal-setting-for-teens-smart-goals/

carolabriney.com » fear. (n.d.). https://carolabriney.com/tag/fear/

Celestine, N., PhD. (2023). 9 Strength finding tests and assessments you can do today. *PositivePsychology.com.* https://positivepsychology.com/strength-finding-tests/

Chen, S. (2018, August 21). *Give yourself a break: The Power of Self-Compassion.* Harvard Business Review. https://hbr.org/2018/09/give-yourself-a-break-the-power-of-self-compassion

Client. (2016a, October 24). *Encouraging Accountability In Teens - Compass Rose Academy.* Compass Rose Academy. https://compassroseacademy.org/encouraging-accountability-in-teens/#:~:text=In%20essence%2C%20boundaries%20and%20accountability,responsibility%20for%20their%20own%20lives.

Clssbb, J. B. D. (n.d.). Do you embrace your individuality? *www.linkedin.com.* https://www.linkedin.com/pulse/do-you-embrace-your-individuality-james-bonner

Coach, S. R. C. L. (n.d.). My story with self-confidence. *www.linkedin.com.* https://www.linkedin.com/pulse/my-story-self-confidence-sandra-rinaldi

Confidence in pre-teens and teenagers. (2021, November 5). Raising Children Network. https://raisingchildren.net.au/pre-teens/development/social-emotional-development/confidence-in-teens

Corp, Z. (2023a, June 5). *Benefits of focusing on strengths in the workplace*. Zaengle Corp. https://zaengle.com/blog/benefits-using-strengths-work

Coursera. (2023a). What is effective communication? Skills for work, school, and life. *Coursera*. https://www.coursera.org/articles/communication-effectiveness

Cpcc, A. K. (2023a). How to Identify Your Strengths and Weaknesses (with Pictures). *wikiHow*. https://www.wikihow.com/Identify-Your-Strengths-and-Weaknesses

Cuncic, A., MA. (2022). What is active listening? *Verywell Mind*. https://www.verywellmind.com/what-is-active-listening-3024343

Darcy, A. M., & Jacobson, S. (2023). Personal accountability – Why you need more of it, now. *Harley Therapy*[TM] *Blog*. https://www.harleytherapy.co.uk/counselling/personal-accountability.htm

Dbojic. (2023, July 8). 72 Positive affirmations for courage: Become more courageous. *Positive Affirmations*. https://positiveaffirmationscenter.com/affirmations-for-courage/

Department of Health & Human Services. (n.d.). *Teenagers and communication*. Better Health Channel. https://www.betterhealth.vic.gov.au/health/healthyliving/teenagers-and-communication

Diggs, K. (2020). 6 ways to embrace your individuality. *aSweatLife*. https://asweatlife.com/2020/12/6-ways-to-embrace-your-individuality/

Dowches-Wheeler, J. (2022). How to overcome limiting beliefs and achieve your goals — Bright Space Coaching | Leadership Development for Women. *Bright Space Coaching | Leadership Development for Women.* https://www.brightspacecoaching.com/blog/how-to-overcome-limiting-beliefs

Effective communication and teenagers - ReachOut Parents. (n.d.). https://parents.au.reachout.com/skills-to-build/connecting-and-communicating/effective-communication-and-teenagers#:~:text=Effective%20communication%20with%20your%20teenager,difficult%20conversations%20and%20resolving%20conflicts.

Embracing individuality: your Self-Expression. (2023, June 6). Maison Septem. https://www.maisonseptem.com/blogs/embracing-individuality-your-self-expression

Engelke, M. (2017). 7 common negative beliefs and the problems they cause. *Liberty Counselling Luxembourg.* https://libertycounsellingluxembourg.com/7-common-negative-beliefs-and-the-problems-they-cause/

Eurich, T. (2023, April 6). *What Self-Awareness really is (and how to cultivate it).* Harvard Business Review. https://hbr.org/2018/01/what-self-awareness-really-is-and-how-to-cultivate-it

Evans, M. (2020a). 5 WAYS TO HELP YOUR TEEN LET GO OF LIMITING BELIEFS — The Teen Coach - Maria Evans. *The Teen Coach - Maria Evans.* https://www.mariateencoach.com/blog/5-ways-to-help-your-teen-let-go-of-limiting-beliefs

Farmer, J. (2023, March 17). *Finding your strengths - Find your natural strengths.* Find Your Natural Strengths. https://pdpfyns.com/finding-your-strengths

Finkelstein, D. (2023). What is personal responsibility? *Tick Those Boxes.* https://tickthoseboxes.com.au/what-is-personal-responsibility/

Fitting in allows you to blend in with everyone else, but being differ. . .- Sonya Parker | Sonya Parker Quotes. (n.d.). Quotss.

http://www.quotss.com/quote/Fitting-in-allows-you-to-blend-in-with-everyone-else-but-being-different-a

Five Ways to Help Teens Feel Good about Themselves. (n.d.). Greater Good. https://greatergood.berkeley.edu/article/item/five_ways_-to_help_teens_feel_good_about_themselves

Forgeard, V. (2022, August 2). Why respect is important - brilliantio. *Brilliantio.* https://brilliantio.com/why-respect-is-important/

Growth, C. F. (2021). Finding your authentic self exercise. *Counseling | Therapy.* https://www.thecenterforgrowth.com/tips/finding-your-authentic-self-exercise

Guiding teens to their authentic identity. (n.d.-a). https://www.nickersoninstitute.com/blog/guiding-teens-to-their-authentic-identity

Gupta, S. (2022). How to embrace Self-Acceptance. *Verywell Mind.* https://www.verywellmind.com/self-acceptance-characteristics-importance-and-tips-for-improvement-6544468

Harvard Health. (2016, May 16). *Greater self-acceptance improves emotional well-being.* https://www.health.harvard.edu/blog/greater-self-acceptance-improves-emotional-well-201605169546

Healthdirect Australia. (n.d.). *Self-esteem and mental health.* Signs, Causes and How to Improve | Healthdirect. https://www.healthdirect.gov.au/self-esteem

How do I improve my body image? | Seeds of Hope. (n.d.). Seeds of Hope. https://seedsofhope.pyramidhealthcarepa.com/how-to-improve-your-body-image/

How to be respectful and respected. (2023, August 18). Kids Helpline. https://kidshelpline.com.au/teens/issues/all-about-respect#:~:text=Being%20respected%20by%20important%20people,trust%2C%20safety%2C%20and%20wellbeing.

How to surround yourself with good people in your life | tonyrobbins.com. (2021, December 30). tonyrobbins.com. https://www.tonyrobbins.-

com/stories/business-mastery/surround-yourself-with-quality-people/

iGod. (n.d.). *Reddit - Dive into anything.* https://www.reddit.-com/r/AskReddit/comments/yh9w2/my_low_selfesteem_is_killing_my_social_life_and/

Jacqui. (2022a, August 13). *5 Common limiting beliefs Destroying your self confidence.* Claire Buck Coaching. https://www.clairebuck.com/5-common-limiting-beliefs-that-could-be-destroying-your-self-confidence/#:~:text=Limiting%20beliefs%20are%20firm-ly%20held,your%20confidence%20and%20self%2Desteem.

Katherine, S. (2022, February 4). *Why You Should Surround Yourself With Positive People – Sara Katherine.* Sara Katherine. https://sara-katherine.com/2017/07/positive-people/

Keelan, P. (2022a, February 8). *How to identify your negative core beliefs - Dr. Patrick Keelan, Calgary Psychologist.* Dr. Patrick Keelan, Calgary Psychologist. https://drpatrickkeelan.com/anxiety/identify-nega-tive-core-beliefs/

Kelly, J. (2022). Do you know what these Gen Z slang terms Mean—And where they really come from? In *Dictionary.com.* https://www.-dictionary.com/e/gen-z-slang/

Kenton, W. (2023a). Accountability: definition, types, benefits, and example. *Investopedia.* https://www.investopedia.com/terms/a/accountability.asp

Kristin, & Kristin. (2015, June 11). Exercise 1: How would you treat a friend? - Self-Compassion. *Self-Compassion - Dr. Kristin Neff.* https://self-compassion.org/exercise-1-treat-friend/

Lăpușneanu, D. (2023, August 10). Most Common English Slang Words And Their Meaning. *Mondly Blog.* https://www.mondly.-com/blog/45-popular-slang-words-from-around-the-world-and-their-meanings/

Li, P. (2023). What Is Respect? Definition for Kids and 6 Highly Effective Ways To Teach. *Parenting for Brain*. https://www.parentingfor-brain.com/6-controversial-tips-teaching-kids-respect/

Lifesmartblog. (2014, May 2). *5 Ways to Help Teens Build Self-Awareness*. Time for Excellence. https://lifesmartblog.com/2014/05/02/5-ways-to-help-teens-build-self-awareness/

Mack, S. (2022a). How confidence affects communication, what to avoid and how to improve yours. *ExcellenceXL*. https://excellencexl.com/how-confidence-affects-communication-how-to-improve/

Manson, M. (2023a, May 23). How to overcome your limiting beliefs. *Mark Manson*. https://markmanson.net/limiting-beliefs#:~:text=Limiting%20beliefs%20are%20false%20be-liefs,you%20don%27t%20want).

Marteka. (2019a). 12 ways to recognise Negative thoughts. *Benevolent Health*. https://benevolenthealth.co.uk/12-ways-to-recognise-nega-tive-thoughts/

Marter, J. (2017, December 7). 15 Ways to live Authentically and amazingly. *HuffPost*. https://www.huffpost.com/entry/15-ways-to-live-authentically-and-amaingly_b_6649610

May, K. (2020). How to help your teen break free of limiting beliefs — creative healing. *Creative Healing*. https://creativehealingphilly.com/blog/how-to-help-your-teen-break-free-of-limiting-beliefs

Mba, C. M. P. (2023). How to Practice Self-Compassion: 8 Techniques and tips. *PositivePsychology.com*. https://positivepsychology.com/how-to-practice-self-compassion/

MEd, S. M. M. (2023, March 27). *Powerful communication activities for teens*. Adult ESL Curriculum. https://adulteslcurriculum.com/2022/08/16/powerful-communication-activities-for-teens/

Method, A. P.-. P. (2022, December 23). 8 Steps for Embracing your Uniqueness - Dr. Asha Prasad. *Dr. Asha Prasad*.

https://drashaprasad.com/self-awareness/embrace-your-uniqueness/

Mfa, K. P. (2022). 11 Ways to be a Responsible Teen - WikiHow. *wikiHow*. https://www.wikihow.com/Be-a-Responsible-Teen

Michael, J., & Michael, J. (2017). How to identify your strengths and weaknesses. *Bplans Blog*. https://articles.bplans.com/how-to-identify-your-strengths-and-weaknesses/

Michalowicz, M. (2022). How to figure out your hidden talents. *Business Class: Trends and Insights | American Express*. https://www.americanexpress.com/en-us/business/trends-and-insights/articles/5-ways-to-find-your-hidden-talents/

Middleearthnj. (2017, September 25). *8 Ways to Instill Accountability in Teens*. Middle Earth. https://middleearthnj.org/2017/09/25/8-ways-to-instill-accountability-in-teens/

MindTools | Home. (n.d.-a). https://www.mindtools.com/ay30irc/authenticity

MindTools | Home. (n.d.-b). https://www.mindtools.com/awe5s-ru/developing-self-awareness

MindTools | Home. (n.d.-c). https://www.mindtools.com/ae-jjzul/body-language

Moran, A. (2021, October 27). *10 simple ways to discover your hidden talent*. https://www.careeraddict.com/find-your-talent

Morin, A. (2023a). 7 Ways to Help Teens and Tweens Gain Self-Awareness. *Understood*. https://www.understood.org/en/articles/7-ways-to-help-teens-and-tweens-gain-self-awareness

MSEd, K. C. (2023a). 11 Signs of Low Self-Esteem. *Verywell Mind*. https://www.verywellmind.com/signs-of-low-self-esteem-5185978

MSEd, K. C. (2023b). Understanding body language and facial expressions. *Verywell Mind.* https://www.verywellmind.com/understand-body-language-and-facial-expressions-4147228

MSEd, K. C. (2023c). What is Self-Awareness? *Verywell Mind.* https://www.verywellmind.com/what-is-self-awareness-2795023

OneEighty. (2023). The Importance of Surrounding Yourself with Positivity. *OneEighty.* https://www.one-eighty.org/news/the-importance-of-surrounding-yourself-with-positivity

Only One you (Celebrating uniqueness). (n.d.). TPT. https://www.teacherspayteachers.com/Product/Only-One-You-Celebrating-Uniqueness-2023003

Outreach. (2022, July 29). *Breaking the cycle: negative thought patterns and depression.* Sage Neuroscience Center. https://sageclinic.org/blog/negative-thoughts-depression/

Parenteau, K., & Parenteau, K. (2023). Solar Plexus Chakra affirmations for powerful healing. *Asana at Home Online Yoga.* https://asanaathome.com/solar-plexus-chakra-affirmations/

Parentingteensandtweens. (2022). More Than 30 Positive Affirmations For Your Teen To Help Their Confidence and Mental Health. *parentingteensandtweens.com.* https://parentingteensandtweens.com/more-than-30-positive-affirmations-for-your-teen-to-help-their-confidence-and-mental-health/

Pattemore, C. (2022, December 9). *6 ways to live an authentic life.* Psych Central. https://psychcentral.com/lib/ways-of-living-an-authentic-life

Positive thinking: Stop negative self-talk to reduce stress. (2022, February 3). Mayo Clinic. https://www.mayoclinic.org/healthy-lifestyle/stress-management/in-depth/positive-thinking/art-20043950

Professional, C. C. M. (n.d.). *Fostering a positive Self-Image*. Cleveland Clinic. https://my.clevelandclinic.org/health/articles/12942-fostering-a-positive-self-image

Quoteresearch. (2012, April 30). *No one can make you feel inferior without your consent – quote Investigator®*. https://quoteinvestigator.com/2012/04/30/no-one-inferior/

Rackliffe, C. (2021). 8 Ways to live a More Authentic Life. *Chris Rackliffe*. https://www.crackliffe.com/words/2019/4/24/8-ways-to-live-a-more-authentic-life

rafikGk. (n.d.). *Reddit - Dive into anything*. https://www.reddit.com/r/DecidingToBeBetter/comments/9n1u7b/heres_what_i_learned_from_having_low_selfesteem/

Rebecca. (2021a, January 10). *Dare To Be Different: 10 Ways to Embrace Your Uniqueness - Minimalism Made Simple*. Minimalism Made Simple. https://www.minimalismmadesimple.com/home/dare-to-be-different/

Refresh. (2014). 5 Ways to Improve your Body Image and Self-Esteem. *Oregon Counseling*. https://oregoncounseling.com/article/5-ways-to-improve-your-body-image-and-self-esteem/

Reynolds, N., & Reynolds, N. (2022, August 18). 75 positive Self-Esteem boosting affirmations for teens. *Raising Teens Today*. https://raisingteenstoday.com/75-positive-self-esteem-boosting-affirmations-for-teens/

Robinson, L. (2023a). Effective communication. *HelpGuide.org*. https://www.helpguide.org/articles/relationships-communication/effective-communication.htm

Rogers, T., MA. (2023). How to Discover Your Talents: 15 Steps (with Pictures) - wikiHow. *wikiHow*. https://www.wikihow.com/Discover-Your-Talents

Romano, C. (2023). 13 Ways To Identify Your Talents And Utilize Them. *Lifehack*. https://www.lifehack.org/articles/productivity/10-ways-identify-your-talents-and-utilize-them.html

Sarah, & Sarah. (2013a). 5 Reasons Why Self-esteem is Very Important in Teenagers | California Counseling Group. *California Counseling Group*. https://californiacounselinggroup.com/5-reasons-why-self-esteem-is-very-important-in-teenagers/

Scott, S. (2023). 67 Positive Affirmations for Teens & Young Students. *Happier Human*. https://www.happierhuman.com/positive-affirmations-teens/

Self-Compassion. (2020, July 10). *What is Self-Compassion? - Self-Compassion*. Self-Compassion - Dr. Kristin Neff. https://self-compassion.org/the-three-elements-of-self-compassion-2/

Self-compassion for pre-teens and teenagers. (2021, June 9). Raising Children Network. https://raisingchildren.net.au/teens/mental-health-physical-health/about-mental-health/self-compassion-teenagers

Self-esteem and teenagers - ReachOut Parents. (n.d.). https://parents.au.reachout.com/common-concerns/everyday-issues/self-esteem-and-teenagers#:~:text=Positive%20self%2Desteem%20-for%20teens,a%20healthy%20and%20positive%20future.

Short, E. (2022, May 26). How to Surround Yourself with Good People and Why You Need to. *Mål Paper*. https://malpaper.com/blogs/news/how-to-surround-yourself-with-good-people-and-why-you-need-to

Social Media Victims Law Center PLLC. (2023, August 3). *Social Media's Effects on Self-Esteem | Social Media Victims Law Center*. Social Media Victims Law Center. https://socialmediavictims.org/mental-health/self-esteem/#:~:text=However%2C%20numerous%20studies%20indicate%20that,%2C%20and%20low%20self%2Desteem.

Spidxrcore. (n.d.). *Reddit - Dive into anything.* https://www.reddit.com/r/AskReddit/comments/qx7ol7/people_who_had_low_-self_esteem_before_but_are/

Stacey. (2023). 46 positive affirmations for teachers - Soular Moon. *Soular Moon.* https://soularmoon.com/positive-affirmations-for-teachers/

Staff, D. (2021a, April 23). 10 ways to Practice Positive Self-Talk. *Del. Psych. Services.* https://www.delawarepsychologicalservices.com/post/10-ways-to-practice-positive-self-talk

Sutton, J., PhD. (2023). Authentic Living: How to be real according to Psychology. *PositivePsychology.com.* https://positivepsychology.com/authentic-living/

Teaching responsibility & values. (2020, March 4). Parents. https://www.parents.com/kids/responsibility/volunteering/

Team, Z. (2021). Negative core beliefs: what they are and how to challenge them. *The Couch: A Therapy & Mental Wellness Blog.* https://blog.zencare.co/negative-core-beliefs/

Tewari, A. (2023). 15 Easy & Simple Positive Thinking Exercises To Improve Your Mood. *Gratitude - the Life Blog.* https://blog.gratefulness.me/positive-thinking-exercises/

The importance of Goal-Setting for teens. (n.d.). https://www.bgca.org/news-stories/2022/January/the-importance-of-goal-setting-for-teens

The path to Self-Acceptance. (n.d.). https://www.betterup.com/blog/self-acceptance

Van Edwards, V. (2023a). 5 Powerful Reasons Why Body Language is Important. *Science of People.* https://www.scienceofpeople.com/body-language-important/

Webb, J. (2022). 20 Goal-Setting Activities for High School Students - Teaching expertise. *Teaching Expertise.* https://www.teachingexpertise.com/classroom-ideas/goal-setting-activities-for-high-school-students/

What are limiting beliefs. (n.d.). https://www.betterup.com/blog/what-are-limiting-beliefs

What is Effective Communication | Laurie Brown. (2022, August 23). Laurie Brown Communications. https://lauriebrown.com/guides/communication-skills/what-is-effective-communication/

What is Self-Awareness, and why is it important? (n.d.-a). https://www.betterup.com/blog/what-is-self-awareness

What is Self-Confidence? | HealthyPlace. (2021a, December 24). https://www.healthyplace.com/self-help/self-confidence/what-is-self-confidence

Yugay, I., & Azman, T. (2023). The importance of personal responsibility to success in life. *Mindvalley Blog.* https://blog.mindvalley.com/personal-responsibility/

Printed in Great Britain
by Amazon

38874557R00084